CHANNEL

OF

PEACE

KEVIN TUERFF

This is a work of nonfiction. The events portrayed are from the author's memory and personal experiences. While all the stories in this book are true, some names and identifying details have been changed to protect the privacy of the people involved.

Published by River Grove Books
Austin, TX
www.rivergrovebooks.com

Distributed by River Grove Books

Design and composition by Greenleaf Book Group
Cover design by Greenleaf Book Group
Photo courtesy of Canadian Armed Forces, 103 Search and
Rescue Squadron, 9 Wing Gander

Cataloging-in-Publication data is available.

Print ISBN: 978-1-63299-120-1

eBook ISBN: 978-1-63299-121-8

First Edition

This book is dedicated to the people of Gander, Newfoundland. Twenty-five percent of the net proceeds from the sale of this book will be donated to Gander Refugee Outreach, an organization that brings refugee families from Syria to Canada so they can experience Gander's unique kindness to strangers.

I hope this book is a reminder that we promised to "never forget" the lives tragically lost in America, and the dedication and kindness of first responders and volunteers on 9/11.

CONTENTS

On September 11, 2001, I was mayor of the town of Gander, Newfoundland, population 10,000. After thirty-eight transatlantic airline flights, carrying 6,500 passengers, were diverted here, I declared a state of emergency and asked our residents to help these international travelers. We saw the worst of humanity and the best of humanity, and on the very same day. It was almost too much to absorb as it was happening, but it changed our lives forever.

The author tells his personal story as a stranded airline passenger, along with stories from volunteers who quickly stepped up to help those from more than three dozen countries around the world who needed food, clothing, and shelter. A lot of friendships were developed over five days. We just do good deeds and cherish the memories.

I met Kevin Tuerff in 2011 when he returned to Gander for the tenth-anniversary ceremonies of the 9/11 attacks in America. However, I'd been watching Kevin's Pay It Forward 9/11 initiative since 2002. It was wonderful to see how the actions taken by the residents of Newfoundland inspired him to organize many others to do good deeds for strangers as far away as Texas, year after year.

We never could have imagined our actions would receive so many accolades, including the amazing *Come From Away* Broadway musical, in which the author and I are featured characters.

The message of this book is very important because our world is divided, with an increase in hatred and intolerance. *Channel of Peace: Stranded in Gander on 9/11* is a beautiful story about how a seed of love can be planted within someone, and years later it grows into a beautiful, flowering tree.

I hope that people who read this book will come away with the important message of making kindness part of their daily life, which can change the world. *Channel of Peace* offers suggestions for how you might make the world better with a simple act of kindness for a stranger.

—**Claude Elliott**
Mayor, Town of Gander (1996–2017)
Newfoundland, Canada

It All Starts With Kindness

Everyone born before 1990 has a 9/11 story. Mine is unique because on that tragic day, I was lucky to witness the kindness of strangers. This kindness, in a tiny, remote town of a foreign country, restored my faith in humanity. I've been relentlessly telling this story ever since, because few are aware of it. The events that day changed my life for the better, and I'm certain my story will do the same for others.

For more than fifteen years, the people of Gander have led by example, serving as a channel of peace. They inspired me in 2002 to start a random act of kindness effort on each anniversary of 9/11. Fifteen years later, this tiny town inspired others again by adopting refugee families from Syria. In 2017, my personal story from 2001 was featured with a character role in the Broadway musical *Come From Away*.

Tony-nominated American Theater actor Chad Kimball sings "Make Me a Channel of Your Peace," playing the character Kevin T., inspired by my experience, in the Broadway musical *Come From Away*. PHOTO CREDIT: KEVIN BERNE

CHAPTER 1

September 11th: Stuck on the Tarmac

Returning to America from vacationing in France, my plane's altitude suddenly dropped and we turned sharply to the north. Our transatlantic flight from Paris was scheduled to arrive mid-morning in New York on September 11, 2001. Apparently US airspace was closed and all planes were told to land at the nearest airport. Thirty minutes later, our plane with 250 people aboard would land on an island in the Atlantic Ocean. At the time, I was confused and annoyed by the diversion. But the change in direction was providential. Being stranded on 9/11 transformed my life for the better, and sixteen years later, it has opened my eyes to how we treat strangers among us and across the world.

Immediately after the September 11th attacks, US airspace was closed and my flight over the Atlantic Ocean was diverted to the Canadian island province of Newfoundland and Labrador. PHOTO CREDIT: KEVIN TUERFF

Our family moved often as I grew up, so it's no surprise that I enjoy traveling. My parents were high school sweethearts from Gary, Indiana, who married after my father graduated from college. Soon they moved to Fort Wayne, Indiana, for Dad's first job in the insurance business, and my birthplace. Dad's career bounced me from Indiana to Atlanta, to Nashville, to Louisville, and finally—in fifth grade—to Houston. The majority of my childhood was spent growing up with my three brothers in suburban northwest Houston, where I graduated high school. My next move would take me to Austin, Texas, where I graduated from the University of Texas. After graduating, my friends at the University Catholic Center helped me come out of the closet as gay at age twenty-two.

One of the priests at my church formed a gay men's support group. It made me feel that I wasn't alone and that my sexual orientation didn't mean I should abandon my Catholic faith. I met several men in the group who I have remained friends with for more than twenty-five years. In the early 1990s, our group members were more than members; they became active leaders in the church. Sadly, in 1993, Pope John Paul II wrote a directive to Catholics from the Vatican that proclaimed "the intrinsic evil of the homosexual condition."

By the mid-1990s, hope for expanding support groups for gay Catholics to other churches was completely lost. Local bishops and priests were toeing the Vatican line. Soon, a young college student who attended my church called home to her conservative parents and told them about our group. Her parents reportedly called the Bishop of Austin. I was told that the Bishop called over to the pastor at my church and immediately squashed the gay support group. This political action not only broke up a group of friends united by religion, but it poked a hole in our faith. Most of my friends abandoned the Catholic Church. I tried to stay involved after the group disbanded, but ultimately I stopped attending Mass.

The energy I put into my faith and my local church was shifted into starting a company that promoted good. In 1997, I cofounded and led the nation's first marketing agency focused solely on improving public health and the environment. Starting a new business was scary and exhausting because of the pressure to continually keep new clients coming in the door, making sure employees would always have food on the table with a monthly paycheck. I didn't have time for volunteering with charities, or connecting with friends and neighbors. I worked seven days a week. It paid off. Our firm won the "Don't Mess with Texas" litter prevention campaign with a staff of four, beating out national ad agencies. I wanted to prove that I could be good at doing good, despite what church leaders or others in society thought of me because of my sexual orientation.

In 2001, my longtime partner Evan and I decided to take a much-needed vacation to Europe. I traveled so much for work that I had enough frequent flier miles for two free round-trip tickets to Europe in late summer.

We had a great time, except for Air France losing our luggage for the first two days of our trip. We went to the store and bought cheap T-shirts. We spent our time discovering the South of France, Amsterdam, and Brussels. On our last day, we took the bullet train from Brussels to Paris, staying the final night at a nice hotel near Charles de Gaulle International Airport.

Our flight left early on the morning of September 11, 2001, so we decided to spend a few hours in Paris with a taxi driver serving as our personal tour guide. I had a new Sony mini-DV camera, so I was taking a lot of video throughout our trip. We drove by most of the major monuments, getting out of the car to walk up to some of them. I narrated as we walked, "Here we are, walking toward the Eiffel Tower on September 10th, I believe."

Late the next morning, we transferred from the airport hotel to Charles de Gaulle Airport. The security at the Paris airport was more attentive than at US airports. France had suffered airport terrorist attacks for many years before 2001, so this didn't bother me. Security officials with guard dogs stopped and asked us questions before we could check in at the Air France ticket counter. Air France Flight 004 would fly from Paris to New York. From there, we would transfer to Continental Airlines and fly home to Austin, Texas.

Evan's favorite cocktail was vodka with club soda. His favorite vodka was Grey Goose, which says "a product of France" right on the label. Throughout our vacation in France, Evan tried in vain to order a Grey Goose cocktail. It took us a while to realize that the French only drink wine. We wondered if Grey Goose was truly made in France. Then, as we were about to depart Paris, Evan stepped into a duty-free shop inside the airport. He emerged with a big grin on his face and two large bottles of Grey Goose.

At the gate, our passports were checked repeatedly, but we were allowed to board. Sitting in our economy-class seats, our flight was normal for several hours. Back then, economy class actually had decent meals on international flights. We were served shrimp salad with melon and mint, chicken with Poitou-style sauce and rice, Rondele cheese, and Charentes-style tartlets with wine. They also served free liquor. I ordered a gin and tonic. The flight was smooth and easy. I had never seen the movie *Shrek*, and the airline played that movie on an overhead TV if you purchased a headset. I bought a headset for what I thought would be a two-hour distraction.

. . .

Air France 004 was due into New York/Newark International Airport around 11 a.m. The United States is roughly west of France. At some point after the movie, I looked up at the TV monitor, which was showing a live GPS map. Our plane had changed direction, from west to north. It looked like we were now flying to the North Pole. I wondered, *maybe the GPS has gone haywire?*

Several minutes later, our Air France captain came on the public address system and said something in French. I heard the words "terrorist activity" in English. I looked up at the GPS screen, but the map was flashing back and forth between English and French. The French translation for the Canadian province of Newfoundland is *Terre-Neuve.* I recognized this word on the screen, but I wasn't quite putting the situation together yet.

Okay, we're flying a weird route over Terre-Neuve, I thought. Then the captain came on the PA, in broken English, saying, "Due to a terrorist attack in the United States, we will be landing in Gander."

That's it. *Huh? Where are we landing, and why?*

I asked Evan if he had heard what the captain said. He wasn't paying attention. We were enjoying free drinks as we flew across the Atlantic, so what was happening didn't immediately sink in. When we were told to put our tray tables up for landing in Gander, it was time to sober up.

I later found out, from fellow passenger Sue Riccardelli (who was flying home to New Jersey), that after the announcement a flight attendant said something to another who looked as if she might faint.

As soon as we were low enough to see land, I took out my camera and snapped a photo. Outside my window were huge green trees—and no civilization.

Gander served as a British Air Force base during World War II and is now a small commercial airport. Newfoundland was under British dominion from 1907 to 1949 and then became a province of Canada. In 2001, Canada's constitution was amended to make the province's official name Newfoundland and Labrador. After we landed, we were told we would be staying there for quite a while and perhaps diverting to Montreal or Toronto later that day. We received no specific news about what had caused our diversion beyond what the captain had said. So we waited patiently as the flight attendants continued to ply us with free drinks.

From my window seat, I could see armed police officers stationed at each of the thirty-eight stranded planes. PHOTO CREDIT: KEVIN TUERFF

Around noon, I looked out my window over the wing and saw dozens of wide-body aircraft landing behind us, one after another. I noticed familiar planes: the red and blue of Delta, American, and Continental; and the unfamiliar: the green shamrock of Aer Lingus, El Al, and Hungarian Airways. Soon a Royal Canadian Mounted Police (CMP) officer with an automatic rifle was stationed on the tarmac below the cockpit of each plane. But these officers weren't like what I expected: They weren't on horses and didn't wear red jackets. *Is it possible a hijacker is on our plane, or another one might be sitting on the runway in Gander?*

Over the course of September 11, 2001, thirty-eight jumbo jets landed at Gander, causing quite a challenge for local air traffic controllers. These thirty-eight were a part of the 122

East Coast planes diverted from the North Atlantic to maritime provinces in Canada. The Gander Airport generally saw fewer than a dozen small commercial planes daily. There are no gates with jetways (walkways from plane to terminal) at the Gander Airport. They had a few trucks that drove stairs up to aircraft for deplaning onto the tarmac.

Even so, Gander had a long runway. When it was built, almost all transatlantic planes needed to stop there temporarily for refueling. Later, innovations with large jets would allow larger fuel tanks to fly farther. During World War II, the US military paid Canada to expand their facilities to accommodate air force planes making trips to Europe. Over time, this caused some problems when other planes refueled there. A plane traveling from Russia to Cuba once landed in Gander and allowed passengers to stretch their feet in the terminal. Soon, some Russians had jumped the fence in an effort to escape from Communism by claiming political asylum in Canada.

On our Air France plane, the passengers waited patiently in our seats until it was clear we weren't going anywhere. No truck with a stairway ever arrived. Evan and I would stand and walk up and down the aisles of the aircraft. Other passengers generally stayed quiet in their seats.

Five hours after we landed, the French-speaking captain came over the PA system again. This time, he provided what little information he had. "What we know now is that two aircraft were hijacked and flown into the World Trade Center. Both towers have fallen. The Pentagon was also attacked by a hijacked aircraft."

Evan was smart and knew his history. "That's impossible,"

he said. "In 1945, someone flew a B-25 airplane into the Empire State Building and the building survived just fine. The twin towers can't fall."

"Who could make that up?" I said.

We didn't understand that the planes were jumbo jets recently loaded with tons of gallons of fuel for cross-country flights. The fuel had turned each one into a giant bomb. Evan was always a skeptic. I tended to trust authorities. *Could it be true?*

My mind was spinning, trying to imagine all the chaos in New York City and Washington, DC. *How many people were killed on the airplanes? How many others were killed and wounded? Was it a surprise attack like Pearl Harbor, and if it was, who did it? Was our military elevating our threat level? Were missile silos being opened up, ready to aim and fire? Or was the Pentagon rendered useless by this attack? Were attacks taking place in several countries or just in the United States? How long would this go on? Were we sure our plane didn't have a hijacker on it?*

I looked out my window at another plane landing and prayed an "Our Father." Praying helped. I soon felt calm, even safe, on our plane, even though I didn't have any reason to believe our plane was free of terrorists. I sensed we'd be okay in Gander.

CHAPTER 2

September 11th: The Terrible News

As anxious as we were, Evan and I and many other passengers couldn't see live TV images, hear radio, read a website, or even call anyone to verify the news we'd been told. It was clear there was a crisis in the US, but without seeing TV or reading anything, it was difficult to imagine.

The idea of airplanes purposefully crashing into buildings seemed absurd. I couldn't picture it in my mind. I wondered if there were additional planes headed for landmark buildings across the US.

Around 3 p.m., a woman sitting in the row behind us was starting to have an argument with her husband. After five hours on the tarmac, she wanted off the plane and didn't understand why we weren't being told more details about what was happening in America and whether or not we were going home. She wanted a phone to call her young children in the US, but that wasn't happening. She kept getting louder.

Everyone around her could hear her anxiety and frustration. Her husband tried to quiet her, but that only made her cry harder. Evan turned around and asked if she needed some medication to ease her nerves. The husband declined.

Evan and I agreed that our friends and family would be worried because we were scheduled to fly into New York City that morning. My flip phone was useless for international calls. On our plane, the only passengers making contact with anyone overseas by phone were sitting in first class. Their seats came with satellite phones that were activated by credit card. After hours of hearing a few, uninformative updates from the captain, I walked up to first class and found a man with an empty seat next to him. He was happy to let me sit there and use the phone. I tried calling my parents in Nashville, Tennessee. I tried also calling my office in Austin, Texas. No luck, the calls never connected. I tried calling friends in other time zones. As I swiped my credit card over and over again, I kept hearing the message "All circuits are busy." The country's phone system was overwhelmed.

Later, I would learn that virtually everyone in America was calling everyone they knew to make sure they were okay. I returned to my seat.

Around 5 p.m., I took out my frustration by journaling on the Air France flight menu:

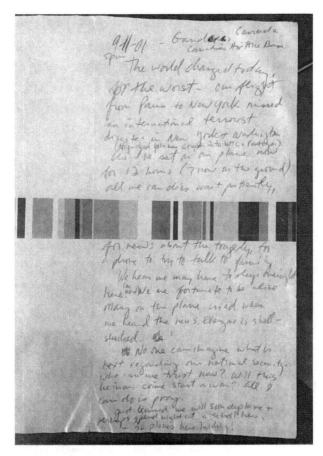

I started journaling on our in-flight menu. PHOTO CREDIT: KEVIN TUERFF

9-11-01-Gander, Canada, Canadian Air Force Base

The world changed today, for the worse. Our flight from Paris to New York missed an international terrorist

disaster in New York and Washington. (Hijacked planes crashed into WTC & Pentagon.)

We've been sitting on our plane now for 12 hours (7 now on the ground). All we can do is wait patiently for news about the tragedy, for a place to try to talk to our families.

We've been told we may have to sleep here overnight (on board). We are fortunate to be alive. Many on the plane cried when we heard the news. Everyone is shell-shocked.

No one can imagine what is next regarding our national security. Who can we trust now? Will this heinous crime start a war? All I can do is pray.

P.S. Just learned we will soon depart plane and perhaps spend night in a school here. At least 30 planes here waiting with stranded passengers aboard.

Around 6:30 p.m. in Gander, it was getting dark outside my window. I walked back up to first class with the idea of calling Europe, instead of the United States. It worked. I reached my high school friend Todd, who lived in Amsterdam, around 11 p.m. Netherlands time. We had just visited Todd a few days earlier on our vacation. That afternoon Todd was walking around Amsterdam with a friend from New York when they heard about the attacks. They decided to go to her house to watch the news. When I reached him, I asked, "Is it true what they're saying?"

"It's horrible," he replied. "I'm watching it live on TV now."

Todd explained that terrorists had hijacked the planes and ultimately destroyed both towers of the World Trade Center, killing thousands. Another plane crashed into the Pentagon, and yet another—which may have been headed to the White House or the Capitol—crashed into a field in Pennsylvania. Early estimates of the dead were nearly 10,000. We didn't know about the plane in Pennsylvania. Tears welled up in my eyes. I was more scared than I could remember, and so was Todd.

I told Todd how I was stuck on the airplane and I couldn't reach anyone in America to let them know I was safe. I asked him to try to call my parents in Nashville and my office in Austin. I also gave him the names and phone number of Evan's parents.

I returned to my coach seat and shared the information with other passengers. Standing up, I spoke to a few people in the row behind me, but soon, dozens of passengers seated within earshot were glued to my every word. Listening to an American confirm that what we had heard from the French pilot was true brought on a deep sense of grief around us. Nobody asked for more details, because they knew I didn't have anything more.

There were passengers on our plane from more than twenty-five countries. Despite such an international melting pot of passengers, everyone seemed to be getting along.

Everyone wondered if they knew someone who might have been harmed.

We felt horrible for the family and friends of the people on those four domestic flights, not to mention the workers and first responders in the World Trade Center and Pentagon. Months later, we would learn that 2,996 people were killed and more than 6,000 injured.

. . .

In all, we sat on the airplane for more than eighteen hours from the time we first boarded in Paris. The crew tried their best to reassure anxious passengers by giving out free liquor and playing and replaying movies on the overhead TV (instead of the GPS screen). For every hour that went by, we kept getting more free drinks, while someone hit rewind to watch *Shrek* for another, agonizing time. It felt strange to laugh at jokes in a movie while New York and Washington were burning. The Leonard Cohen song from the movie, "Hallelujah," kept repeating in my mind in Rufus Wainwright's beautiful voice.

I felt helpless. I wanted to help my fellow Americans, or reach out and talk to friends and family.

Meanwhile, the lack of communication was causing my family stress. My older brother Brian had gone on a Gulf Coast fishing trip with friends in South Texas that day. His boat had headed out before the attacks began, so he didn't know about the tragedy unfolding. His wife Jana desperately tried to reach him about me, but could only call the marina manager. She told the manager to let Brian know what was happening as soon as he returned and to tell him that I was okay. When Brian's boat arrived late that afternoon, the marina manager anxiously greeted my brother and got the story backward. He told Brian, "Your brother was on a plane. Planes crashed into the World Trade Center. But, he's okay."

Brian freaked out, thinking I was killed during my flight. My parents and my brother in Nashville saw the attacks on the news. Fortunately, my brother Greg was able to access the Air France website, which showed our status as having landed in Gander, Newfoundland. They had to look up on a map to see where that was in Canada.

Greg was able to contact Jana, so that later, when Brian called Jana, she clarified that I was safe in Canada. By this time, all flights were canceled, so Brian and his friends rented the last car in South Texas and drove straight home to Austin, arriving five hours later.

If I were at home in Austin, I would certainly be at the office, glued to the television. At my company in Austin, there was a lot of anxiety. Both company principals were traveling that day, one returning from a trip to the US Open in New York City, and me, returning from Europe through New York. Sara Beechner, the manager on duty, was getting ready for work when her fiancé called her into the living room to watch the attacks on live TV. She recalls, "I remember the optimist in me thought, 'What a horrible accident. How could someone accidentally crash a plane into the tower?' I just couldn't compute it to be terrorism; I didn't understand the gravity of the situation. I had to get into the office."

Valerie Davis, the other company principal, landed safely in Austin. She had been on one of the last planes to leave New York before the attacks, and one of the last in the air before the airspace was shut down. Sara later told me, "We got word Valerie was safe, so we were just trying to figure out, 'Where in the hell is Kevin Tuerff?'"

Staff were in shock because news reports were unfolding that other planes in the air could be potential missiles all across the country, and there was no way I could reassure them that I was okay.

Thankfully, my friend Todd was successful at contacting my friend and colleague Sara in Austin and letting her know Evan and I were safe in Gander. Sara took it from there, calling both sets of our parents. They were relieved to know we were okay, even after they had seen the flight updates.

More than eleven hours after we landed in Gander, plus the six more from when we traveled from Paris, we actually left the plane.

Our captain had no information about where we would be going except that it was a shelter. But he told us we could not take our luggage, only our carry-on bags. Authorities were fine with screening passengers, but there was fear that luggage might contain bombs.

Were we going to a refugee camp with tents and cots? Should we take pillows and blankets? I wondered. Unsure of what we were in for in this tiny town of Gander, Evan and I spotted and swiped a full, sealed bottle of Evian water from the flight attendant cart as we deplaned. In our carry-on bags, we had three cameras, two passports, and two sorely needed bottles of vodka.

CHAPTER 3

September 11th–12th: Where Am I and Who Are These Nice People?

*"Everybody is from somewhere else in Newfoundland,
but if you're a traveler from somewhere else,
you're a 'come from away.'"*

—Newfoundland folklore

After finally stepping off the plane, walking down the stairway onto the tarmac, I felt a great sense of relief. It was around 9 p.m. It was dark and the air temperature felt cool, considering we were both wearing shorts. I turned my camera on, capturing the airport's Gander sign. I spoke into the microphone, "We're free, we're free! After I-don't-know-how-many hours on that awful plane, we're free. We don't know where we're going, but we're going."

I turned the camera to Evan. He said, "We're in Gander, and all I know is they better have CNN here."

Inside the airport, security was very serious and tight, and there were just two Canadian immigration and customs authorities available to check passports. The airport staff would work nonstop around the clock for days to deplane the 6,500 stranded passengers. After the screening, we entered the main terminal, which was a little bigger than a high school auditorium.

That's when the first wave of unconditional love hit us: The terminal was filled with volunteers greeting us as we registered. It was like we had walked into a party! There were dozens of volunteers present. Some were wearing their Salvation Army or Red Cross uniforms, sitting at ten-foot-long tables. Their job was to make sure every stranded passenger was documented and taken care of. Most of them were older adults, perhaps looking a bit Irish, like me. There were dozens of volunteers at tables set up with food (from home-baked goods to Kentucky Fried Chicken).

The Air France flight crew had distributed all the food they had, so we weren't hungry. Thinking we might be headed to a tent camp, Evan and I grabbed food and drinks, unsure of when we might be fortunate enough to have these items again. We were told to immediately head outside to a waiting school bus that would take us to our shelter.

Just then, I spotted a pay phone (remember those?) inside the terminal. I grabbed it and dialed an international collect call to my parents in Nashville, Tennessee. They'd been sitting nervously by the phone for more than a dozen hours, waiting to hear from me.

I heard the operator dial the number, and then I heard my mom's voice say, "Hello?" The operator said, "I have an international collect call from Kevin, will you accept the charges?" She did.

"Hello?" I said. Dad picked up another phone at home so he could join in. "It's so great to hear your voice," he said.

I immediately started to cry after hearing their voices. Mom also choked up, but said, "It's okay, it's okay to cry."

"I'm in Iceland or Nova Scotia," I said.

My dad quickly said, "No, we've been tracking you. We know where you are. You're in Gander."

"Is that Iceland?" I asked.

"No, you're on an island called Newfoundland in Canada," my dad pronounced it *New-found-land*. I would soon find out it's pronounced *Newfinland*.

"What in the hell is going on?" I asked. "We haven't seen any TV."

"Four planes were hijacked and crashed into buildings, exploding like bombs. New York and Washington are in complete chaos," Dad replied. "It's unbelievable."

Almost as soon as I began talking to my parents, a local volunteer told me I needed to hang up the phone or I would miss my bus to the shelter.

"Mom, Dad, I have to go," I said. "I love you."

Immediately after I got off the phone, the volunteers must have realized they would never get the passengers off the planes promptly if everyone tried to call home at airport pay phones. As Evan and I walked off, I saw them tape a fake sign on the pay phones that said "out of order." I felt bad for the passengers behind me who had family and friends in New York and Washington. For some, it would be another twenty-four hours or more before they could deplane in Canada.

We loaded onto a school bus and off we went into the darkness.

. . .

The town of Gander managed a massive volunteer effort in a matter of a few hours. At midday, the town council declared a state of emergency and Mayor Claude Elliott went on local TV and radio to urge everyone in this town of 10,000 to help out their unexpected 6,500 guests.

The people of Gander heeded Mayor Elliott, often deciding to do something before they heard the mayor's call to action.

Diane Davis, a teacher at Gander Academy, remembers driving down to see the planes at the airport that afternoon. She recalls, "Traffic was bumper to bumper past the end of one runway. Police directed cars of curious locals past. Planes, huge passenger planes, were nose to tail or side by side, with some of their wing tips overlapping. Some planes had open doors, which indicated its passengers were still aboard, with police cruisers circling the taxiways."

After seeing the magnitude of how many people were stranded, Diane thought she could do something, so she went to the town hall to volunteer. Soon, she'd be co-managing a school-turned-shelter with more than 700 people sleeping on the floors.

Nellie Moss and her husband Mac were at home watching the news when he got the call from the town emergency operations center that airline passengers would be sent to the College of the North Atlantic, across the street from the power company where Nellie worked. Mac was the top administrator at the college.

The power company immediately sent employees to pick up groceries to distribute to schools that were turning into refugee shelters. The company paid for all the expenses. But that was just the start.

"Mac told me, 'Well, we have to look for bedding, pillows, whatever,'" Nellie remembers.

Nellie called her friends, and they called their friends, and then their friends did the same, creating a snowball effect. "In an hour or less, I had my car filled with bedding and I was on my way to the college. I remember taking everything in my house—everything except what was on my bed."

Mac recalls, "I got the call from the Gander emergency communications center that we should expect the flight of 250 Air France passengers to arrive around 8:30 p.m. So I called my key team. They volunteered to lead certain tasks. Half a dozen guys were stringing cable so we could provide the passengers with cable TV. We had people clearing classrooms to make space for people to sleep on the floor. We didn't get any cots from the military until three days later. The college had our cooking staff, which ran the culinary program. We had them and some students go to the store to get whatever groceries they could lug home, so we could get a meal and a breakfast for everyone. We were busy until everyone arrived around 10 p.m."

Before long, thanks to the work of people like Nellie, Mac, and Diane, all public buildings, churches, and schools in Gander had been converted to shelters. Gander's three hotels were emptied out so that the airline pilots and crew from the thirty-eight planes could stay there to rest. Supermarkets and fast-food restaurants donated all the food they could, without asking who was paying the bill.

. . .

The driver of our school bus told me, Evan, and the other passengers he was taking us to the College of the North Atlantic. The ride from the airport to the college was less than fifteen minutes. However, the driver didn't give any commentary about where we were, or information about what to expect. It might have been helpful to know they had a Walmart, Subway sandwiches, and Kentucky Fried Chicken. Gander was a tiny town, but it was hardly a third-world country.

After getting off the school bus, we walked through the dark, into the community college. It was empty except for the new strangers from Air France and dozens of local volunteers. We were funneled into the cafeteria, where they had plenty of food and drinks, plus they had what we really wanted: TV news. At one end of the cafeteria was a TV tuned to a French-speaking news network, and at the other end was a TV tuned to CNN in English.

At the college, donations of food and bedding continually poured in all night from individuals. It was like we had landed at a free buffet with cod au gratin (fish and cheese casserole), doughnuts, hot dogs, soft drinks, and more.

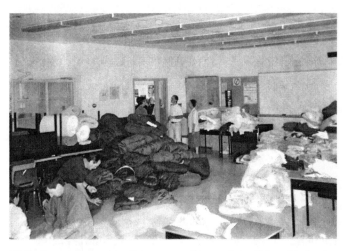

Within hours, a community college was turned into a refugee shelter with sleeping bags and pillows donated by Gander residents. PHOTO CREDIT: MAUREEN MURRAY

The Salvation Army and Red Cross did an amazing job that first night. Within an hour of our Air France plane arriving, the Salvation Army showed up with a Ziploc bag for each passenger, each filled with a feminine sanitary napkin, toothbrush, and toothpaste.

The college had three nurses on staff. It was their job to intercept passengers as they checked in, to identify whether any refugee had medical needs. There were a lot of diabetics and people with high blood pressure. They had all their medications in their checked bags, which had all been left on the plane. If a passenger had an issue, the nurses went to local pharmacists, who were working around the clock, and brought back everything requested. Passengers asked how much they should pay, but were told it was free.

Around midnight, I spotted a teenage boy walking in the front door, carrying a double-sized air mattress and two pillows. Knowing an air mattress would be nicer than sleeping bags, I ran over to meet him. Until that time, I had never been in a situation in my life where I needed a hand from a stranger.

It wasn't that I couldn't afford a hotel room—there were no rooms. I was always a problem solver, but at this moment, I had to rely on the kindness of strangers to help me with my basic needs. In the Bible, it's written, "For I was hungry and you gave me food, I was thirsty and you gave me drink, I was a stranger and you welcomed me" (Matthew 25:35). This was happening from the people of Gander, with little encouragement. As the teenager gave me his bedding, a lump of gratitude rose in my throat. I said, "Thank you."

"You betcha," the young man said in his Canadian accent before turning and walking back out the door.

I was tired, so I went to find my partner, but Evan wasn't ready for bed. He was glued to the TV, watching the images of the planes hit the World Trade Center again and again, surrounded by other passengers. By this time, it was clear that thousands of people, including first responders, had been killed. We were in shock, understanding later than the rest of the world what had happened on this horrific day.

We comforted ourselves with the buffet line in the cafeteria. At one point, I turned on the camera to capture Evan chomping on a hot dog with mustard oozing out of it. I jokingly (and incorrectly stating our location) said to the camera, "Wow, we had to come all the way to Nova Scotia to get a hot dog."

But we were shaken. Underneath our laughter, our nerves

were on edge. So we turned to other comfort: our stash of Grey Goose vodka.

I commandeered a space in a classroom, blowing up the double air mattress. I wondered how other passengers would feel about two men sleeping together on the same air mattress. While Evan and I had been out of the closet for several years, I didn't know what to expect in a small town in another country.

Evan and I finally went to sleep around 2:30 a.m. The wonderful air mattress had a leak in it, so soon after lying on it, we heard the air flowing out until we lay on the cold tile floor and pulled the sheet across us. Shortly thereafter, someone in the room vomited, perhaps from all the free booze on the airplane. The stench was awful, so we hauled our air mattress, sheets, and pillows to another classroom.

As we settled in to sleep, I was happy that I wasn't alone on this trip. It was exhausting and scary.

. . .

While Evan and I slept, the town of Gander was on the move. Unknown to me, thousands of Gander residents were working to help us. Many, including Mayor Elliott, would not sleep for several days. At times, it seemed like all 10,000 men, women, and children in town were volunteering in some capacity. Retail clerks and pharmacists worked around the clock. High school media teacher and part-time Rogers TV reporter Brian Mosher logged twenty-seven straight hours helping passengers, by cooking breakfast at Gander Collegiate, the local high school. Just as he was trying to go to bed at 9 a.m. on September 12th, he was called to the TV station. He went on the air immediately, playing a key role conveying to locals what the needs were at different shelters. Brian was amazed how quickly people responded to specific requests for food, toiletries, and clothing. He worked three live shows per day for the next four days, running back and forth between the school and the station. "Sleep was basically short catnaps, and there weren't many of those," he said. Telephone company workers set up temporary phone banks. Everyone with a kitchen started cooking.

After Gander was filled to capacity with refugees, even smaller towns nearby like Gambo, Lewisporte, and Appleton stepped up to help. Local bus drivers who were on strike left the picket lines to help transport passengers thirty miles or more each way during the emergency.

Mac and Nellie Moss lived one house down from her sister Sue and her husband Ron Walsh, who were also a part of the volunteer effort. Sue was the first to put her bedding into Nellie's car. Years later Sue would tell me, "We wrote our names on our pillows, hoping we'd get them back after this was over."

After all the refugees had left, Sue Walsh and the other people who had donated bedding went back to the school and everything they had loaned was there. "We washed everything, put it on the line, and all was good," Sue remembers. "Some people said, 'Well, I don't want mine back. I'll throw it out because some stranger used it.' But I thought, 'Some poor stranger had to sleep on my bedding.'"

Ron volunteered at Gander Collegiate. They asked him to arrive at 4 a.m. since their first plane was only deplaning in the middle of the night. When he arrived, there were some other men there from the Lions Club. They asked him to help scrub the floors so everything would be clean when the "plane people" arrived. Next, they asked him to help make breakfast. Ron's job was to make toast. Classes at the college were cancelled until further notice, so he didn't have to worry about sleeping late on the floor while students arrived for class.

Sue was working at the Gander Credit Union that same day. She remembers how a come from away Irish couple came in for a currency exchange. They had saved up to take a large group of kids to Disney World. Their shelter was a Salvation Army camp about thirty minutes from Gander. They told her that the kids weren't disappointed at all at being diverted to Newfoundland; in fact, they were having fun. "The kids saw a bear and they thought they really were visiting Disney World," Sue said.

. . .

Back at the College of the North Atlantic, I was getting up as the sun rose, brightening the classroom. The rest of the passengers woke, but Evan kept on sleeping. His snores were so loud, I laughed. Thankfully, classes were canceled.

When he finally got up, we knew we needed some supplies. After spending all day in our clothes on the plane, plus sleeping in them, we were desperate for a change of underwear and socks, at a minimum. We asked around and were told there was a Walmart about three miles away.

It was a beautiful day, so Evan and I decided to walk there. But, we didn't make it more than twenty-five yards down the road when a car pulled up next to us and rolled down the window.

"Where do ya need to go?" the driver asked.

We explained we needed clothes from Walmart.

"Hop in!"

So we did. The driver dropped us off, refusing money. It was my first experience as a hitchhiker.

Inside the Walmart were hundreds of stranded passengers. When we arrived at the men's underwear aisle, several men, including some elderly ones, stared at the emptied-out shelves as if they couldn't believe that underwear was so important. The standard-issue white briefs were gone, except for odd sizes. All that remained were bikini briefs and boxer shorts. Evan and I quickly grabbed some boxers, a package of white T-shirts, and tube socks.

Without our luggage, we went to Walmart in Gander to purchase new underwear, T-shirts, and socks. PHOTO CREDIT: KEVIN TUERFF

After we checked out, we started walking back to the college and once again a stranger stopped and asked where they could take us. Every person we came across was kind, friendly, and sympathetic about what had happened to America.

The College of the North Atlantic was a fantastic facility to be stranded in. Aside from having many classrooms that had been converted into sleeping rooms, the college also had working phones. These were made available so every passenger could call their families around the world as often as they'd like, at no charge, even though the bill to the college would total thousands of dollars. The college also had a computer lab people could use to send email to their loved ones and read news.

Best of all, the college offered a commercial cooking program with a full kitchen. On the third night at our shelter, the volunteers whipped up 200 stuffed chicken breasts for dinner. It tasted better than any meal we had been served at any restaurant on our European vacation.

How did they suddenly find 200 chickens on short notice in a tiny town? I couldn't help but be reminded of the Gospel stories of "feeding the multitudes" where Jesus took five loaves of bread and two fish and performed a miracle that fed the 5,000 people who had gathered for his sermon—and still had leftovers.

Sixteen years later, I finally learned how this mini-miracle happened. Marine cooking instructor Elizabeth Moss told me, "When we got word passengers were coming on the afternoon of September 11th, head chef Barry Steele, myself, and two of my kids went shopping at all three grocery stores in Gander to find enough chicken. We charged all costs to the college, without limit. We bought enough chicken, plus other meat for sandwiches, and soup."

She added, "Our culinary students had just begun, so they hadn't been trained in the kitchen yet. Still, they were a big help to us as volunteers."

Food donations began pouring in so quickly from church parishioners and general public that there was no room for keeping food cold. In response, Mayor Elliott declared the town's ice hockey rink "the world's largest walk-in refrigerator."

Meanwhile, at Gander Collegiate, two passengers were identified as world-famous chefs. One fellow was from India, where he was a top chef at a resort in the Azores. Another man was head chef from a group of hotels. Ron Walsh was there in the kitchen, trying to help them.

"Neither one of them would let us help," he said. "They just said, 'No, no, this our treat this time.'"

The chefs took over the small kitchen, telling the volunteers what food they needed, including spices. The volunteers brought back everything they needed in no time.

It felt like every stove in the Gander area was on, cooking nonstop for the come from aways. They baked Newfoundland dishes, moose stew, or cupcakes, but they all made the same thing: comfort food.

. . .

Evan and I were fortunate that we didn't have to sleep overnight on the parked airplane, like some of the other refugees did. Passengers like Nick Marson and Diane Kirschke.

Nick, from the United Kingdom, and Diane, from Houston,

were both traveling alone on Continental Flight 05 when they were diverted to Gander. After they woke on the morning of September 12th, airport officials sent breakfast out to their plane. They spent a total of twenty-five to twenty-eight hours on their aluminum tube before deplaning into the Gander Airport. Passengers were greeted by Red Cross volunteers, who gathered pertinent information and ensured that passengers would have a well-organized return to their individual planes when the emergency was over.

Nick and Diane were separated from the rest of the Continental flight because they needed medication; their medication was in the checked luggage. Pharmacists worked around the clock for two days filling prescriptions. Subsequently, medication was delivered to each shelter. Diane went with a volunteer to the Salvation Army shelter in Gander, where she was given hot soup and sandwiches. Nick went via a school bus directly to the Society of United Fishermen (SUF) Hall in Gambo, a thirty-four-minute drive. The Salvation Army shelter was full, so Diane was taken by a volunteer to the SUF in Gambo.

The volunteers in Gambo went to the Canadian Army to retrieve cots and blankets for more than eighty visitors. More than a dozen volunteers helped out at all times, with four men spending the night to help with whatever needs the passengers had. Nick and Diane met while waiting in line for their military-issue blankets. Diane smelled her blanket and said, "Oh my, mothballs."

Nick laughed and explained that "camphor" is the term the British use for mothballs.

Since she seemed friendly to him, he asked if he could

camp next to her cot. She agreed. After hours of watching the images from New York and Washington on TV, they had had enough. They joined a married couple on a walk down the gravel road to see Gambo. The other couple turned back because the wife was wearing heels and couldn't manage the rocky road. After walking a while, Nick and Diane stopped at a small convenience store to buy a beverage. Nick was stunned when Diane paid for his drink.

"As a gentleman, I'd always been the one to pay," Nick would later tell me. "Who was this woman who did *this*?"

Nick liked Diane's assertiveness, so he ended up spending the rest of his time while in Gambo with her. After being so close over a few days, they both found they had feelings for each other. The spark for romance between two strangers was kindled in Gambo. Nick transferred to Texas, where they were married. They returned to Newfoundland for their honeymoon in September 2002, which coincided with the first anniversary of 9/11.

. . .

Next door at the high school, Ron Walsh got to meet people from everywhere. He really enjoyed speaking to the international passengers from a Lufthansa flight and a Continental Airlines flight. But he noticed that there was one Arab family—a husband, wife, and little girl—that were unnerved.

"Only the husband spoke a bit of English. They were by themselves, alone all of the time. I went over to introduce myself anyway. I made sure they were comfortable," Ron remembered.

"They were the loneliest people there. The word was already coming out on the news that these attacks were probably linked to Osama bin Laden. I thought, 'That little girl has nothing.' So I went down to Walmart and I found this sweet little plush blue teddy bear. I went back to the school and told the father, 'I have this gift for your little girl.' The husband agreed it was okay to give it to her. The wife and I cried. Then, every time they would come down to the cafeteria for a meal, they would come see me. They felt safe with me as their contact."

At Gander Academy, the town's elementary school, an Egyptian woman who lived in Gander brought vegetarian food because she knew Muslims might be passengers on the planes and they often don't eat meat unless it comes from a Muslim butcher. While at the school, she started to cry because she heard that one of the hijackers in the US was Egyptian. She worried about discrimination and retaliation against Muslims.

Meanwhile, one of the Muslim airline refugees was so moved by the kindness of strangers that he asked the librarian where he could buy a plaque in Gander, to present it as a thank-you. The librarian told him about a local marble shop and helped him with his English for the inscription. The man went out and paid to have the plaque done while he was still there. It read—

"To the students and teachers of Gander Academy, thank you for sharing your school."

He called everyone together at the school to present it to the principal, on behalf of all the passengers. The plaque still graces the wall of the library.

Gander Academy housed hundreds of stranded passengers from four different planes. Diane Davis remembers how heart-wrenching it was to see people watching TV news reports of the attacks, to see their reaction as footage showed the towers getting hit over and over again.

. . .

On September 12th, I successfully placed a call back to my office in Austin. The staff had assembled in the conference room and I spoke to everyone via speakerphone. They helped me better understand the national magnitude of what had happened. All US airspace was still shut down and nobody, including the airlines, knew how long it would be closed. Businesses had shut their doors out of fear of additional terror attacks. It was serious. One person said, "I don't think you understand. There is no advertising running on any TV station and almost every cable TV station is showing nothing but news about the attacks."

The conference room at my office turned into a crisis war room. Normal business had been shut down; this war room had one objective: Get me home. Each staff member was researching some way to do just that. A world map was posted on the wall with a big circle drawn around Newfoundland. Someone researched ferry service from Newfoundland to Maine. Because every rental car in the US was taken, another researched how to buy a car for me to pick up at the US-Canadian border. But even the borders were closed. I was grateful to have such caring, resourceful people helping me remotely.

At lunch that day, I had a remarkable small-world

connection. I turned to a nice woman sitting across from me and introduced myself.

"Where are you from?" I asked.

"New Jersey," she said.

"What do you do there?" I asked.

"I own a PR agency," she said.

"Wow. I own a PR agency," I said. "Who are some of your clients?"

"One of our biggest clients is a company called Trex. They make outdoor decks from a composite of wood and recycled plastic," she said.

"I know Trex! We just bought a Trex deck for our backyard. My PR firm focuses on environmental issues. In fact, one of our clients is America Recycles Day. I remember talking to someone two years ago about a donation of Trex for a national contest. We built and gave away the American Green Dream Home," I said.

"Uh, that was ME you spoke to!" she said.

Maureen Murray and I couldn't believe we had spoken by phone several times to arrange a publicity photo and had briefly met at a trade show. Later, she remembered we had briefly met at a convention two years before and she'd taken a picture of me with her client. But there we were, stranded in Gander, sitting at a cafeteria table at the College of the North Atlantic. We had even more in common.

Maureen introduced me to her partner, Sue Riccardelli. I introduced them both to Evan.

At Gander Academy, someone delivered a giant box of men's underwear. Diane went on the school's intercom to announce, "We just had a box of men's underwear delivered.

If you want some underwear, please line up at the counselor's office. For all you Brits on Virgin 21, that's knickers."

Although Diane was working nonstop at the school, she offered strangers access to her home across the street, to go inside to take a shower. She told two women wearing traditional African dresses to use her home.

"When they returned, they told me, 'We knocked and knocked and nobody answered.' The door was unlocked. So I had to walk them across the street to assure them they could go inside."

Also at the academy, an elderly passenger was exasperated trying to reach his son who worked in the World Trade Center. He needed help, so he went to the best resource expert around: the librarian. The man had a business card for his son, which showed an address in the World Trade Center. She interviewed him about all the facts, and she tried calling a number of agencies in New York City. They had no luck when they first tried to locate him. Two days later, the man finally remembered his ex-daughter-in-law's name. The librarian found her name in directory assistance and called her. Thankfully, she said she had spoken with the man's son. Although the son was in the World Trade Center at the time of the attacks, he had made it out safely.

CHAPTER 4

September 13th: We Stink and
We Want to Go Home

There were no showers at the college, so we began to stink. Evan and I met volunteer Terry Dechman, who worked at the college. She and another coworker volunteered to drive us to the military base athletic facility, which was offering passengers use of their showers. Afterward, they drove us around the airport. It looked like an airplane graveyard because it had so many planes but none of the noise or fumes of jet engines.

Standing outside the airport fence, within view of our quiet Air France plane, I recorded an interview with Terry on my video camera. I asked her, "So, what's it like having all these visitors?"

She replied, "Actually, it's been kind of fun. I work at the College of the North Atlantic, and that day (9/11) we had an emergency meeting at 3 p.m., and we were told we would be bedding down some of the passengers. Everyone got into the spirit of things, I think.

"I got a call at 7:30 that night to go up to the college. We were told Air France passengers would arrive at 8:00, but they didn't get there until 10 p.m."

She paused for a moment.

"You could see they were absolutely stunned by what had happened. One of the things that was really helpful we did was set up several TVs in the cafeteria. They didn't have any information. I was amazed by how absorbed they were in seeing what happened in America twelve hours before.

"I took a family home with me. I identified a family with a young child, about eighteen months. I myself have traveled with an infant, and I know how difficult it can be. They were from Burlington, Vermont. So, I got to know one family quite well."

By late afternoon on Thursday, September 13th, signs were posted around the college announcing a passenger meeting with the crew. Up to that point, several of us had wondered where the airline crew was. We had had no updates from Air France at all since leaving the plane. Everyone gathered in the school cafeteria. Captain Hollande spoke first in French, then in broken English. The head flight attendant spoke in German, and another flight attendant spoke in Italian.

"We are very touched by this college and their kindness that we have received here. We are very touched by it," they said. The passengers applauded. An unknown passenger created a donation box using an old cardboard box. A teenager wrote "scholarship fund" on it, using black magic marker.

She and a friend passed the box around the cafeteria, just like you'd see during a collection in church. Evan and I dropped US dollars in the box, while others added foreign currency. We later learned thousands of dollars were donated that day, which was used to start a scholarship fund at the college.

"Now for the future: We didn't meet you before now because we didn't have any serious information to give. Now we know we will leave tomorrow morning. We are supposed to leave; we hope to leave. I don't know at what time. It won't be early, so you can sleep as much as you want. You will be informed in time.

"There are two possibilities: The first is that we fly to New York; the second, we fly to Paris."

When the captain said this, there were audible gasps of confusion.

"We will make our choice based on what will be the shortest way. For those that want to fly to New York, perhaps it will be shorter to fly to Paris and then come back, because the airspace will be open in New York in thirty-six hours. If that's the case, we bring everyone back to Paris. Then you find a way back to New York. I don't know if this is very clear for you. I hope so. We thought we could fly to Montreal, but in fact, it won't be considered."

"It doesn't make sense to fly all the way back to Paris!" someone said.

The French captain attempted to explain. "The first point is to go to New York. That's what we are trying to do. But if the airport is not open for another thirty-six hours, we will surely go back to Paris, then fly from Paris to New York."

"What?!" a woman yelled out.

An American man screamed, "That's burning a lot of gas!"

An Italian man said in accented English, "That is unusual. That is unusual."

The German flight attendant tried to calm the crowd. "First we have to respect the US authorities. They do not allow us to change the passengers, or to change aircraft. So you are coming with us! And you will go with us to New York, if we can. If they tell us you can wait five or ten hours to go to New York, we'll wait. But if they tell us you must wait five to ten hours to go back to Paris, and then another thirty-six hours to go to New York, we will go back to Paris, because it will be easier for you to get a room in the hotel in Paris. Then you can catch the first flight to the US or whatever destination.

"For example, there is a woman here who is trying to go to Atlanta. I think it is better for her to go back to Paris, then take the next flight from Paris to Atlanta. There is no question. What are you going to do in New York? The security measures and procedures are so extreme in New York that you are going to spend hours to check out and change aircraft. This is not a question. So the best way for many passengers going to New York and other places is through Paris. That's a fact."

The language barrier made this very confusing. We didn't want to go back to anywhere in Europe at a time when war had broken out. What if the attacks started again when the airspace reopened? What if the US decided to take weeks before allowing anyone to fly into the country? We wanted to wait it out in Gander until US airspace reopened.

Back at the college, Evan and I went to the computer lab to email my office about this latest news. If we went back to Paris, would we really be on our way back to Austin in a few days? Or could this attack be the start of an immediate counterattack, an all-out war, which would leave us stuck in Paris? In some ways, being stranded in Paris didn't sound that bad—unless war immediately broke out. What if we were stuck there for a month or longer? I had clients I needed to get back to.

The email reply came back, "Don't go back to Paris!"

I remember approaching Mac Moss to inquire about other options for getting to the US besides air travel.

"Well, there's a bus that goes once per day to the west coast of Newfoundland, that takes six hours," Mac began. "Then you could catch a ferry across the Atlantic Ocean to Nova Scotia. You should know the seas might be rough because there's a hurricane brewing down to the south. That ferry takes nine hours."

He paused for a second before continuing. "From there, you might be able to catch a bus to the train in Halifax. You can take the train from Halifax to the US border at St. Croix, Maine, assuming the border is open by then.

"Then you'd have to drive to Austin," he finished, "if you can find a rental car or a bus or train."

Without including stops, it would take fifty-seven hours to get to Austin, Texas, and would take two and a half days just to get to the US border. All of this would cost well over $3,000 for both of us.

Then came the false alarm.

News came out that the airspace would be reopened, so we were given a couple hours of notice to be prepared to board school buses back to the airport. Flight crews also got dressed and went to the airport, ready to go at a moment's notice. Then something happened.

As it turned out, US airspace was not yet reopened. Word got back to passengers that we were not leaving yet. They told us they would give us a four-hour notice. So we could go wherever we wanted, but we had to stay close to our Gander home in case new departure instructions came out.

American Airlines captain Beverley Bass had a telling experience during this "false alarm." She and her crew were dressed and ready to go at the Gander Airport when they heard the news about the additional delay. They would return to the Comfort Inn, which was now beginning to feel like home to them. There really isn't a significant taxi service in Gander, and no one was around to give them a ride.

Beverley's team was frustrated, standing curbside at the airport, just waiting. At that moment, Beverley looked around and noticed two elderly women approaching them. One of the women, sensing their anxiety, opened up her bag and pulled out an accordion. She began to play "God Bless America."

"There wasn't a dry eye in the crowd," she said. A foreigner serenading a group of Americans with a patriotic song was so moving in light of the crisis in America. I wonder if Americans would do the same for Canadians if they were stranded in the US?

. . .

Back at the College of the North Atlantic, people decided to get outside to take advantage of the beautiful weather. A group of teenagers were playing a game of soccer. It was a pickup game that included the Costa Rican rafting team and some Americans and Europeans. Everyone was having fun and getting along.

After overdosing on TV news of the World Trade Center, many passengers decided to spend time outdoors on the lawn of the College of the North Atlantic campus in Gander. PHOTO CREDIT: MAUREEN MURRAY

Evan and I were sitting in a second-floor classroom, watching the game, when we met Ted, an older gentleman from our flight. He was an American who lived full-time in Paris. He had been traveling to New York City to put his apartment up for rent.

"Where is your apartment?" I asked him.

"Lower Manhattan," Ted replied.

We sat for a moment before Ted explained that the apartment wasn't adjacent to the World Trade Center, but it was nearby.

"I wonder if it's been demolished in the attacks," he sighed.

About this time, Sue and Maureen dropped by. Sue asked, "Do you want to go on a walk with us and two other ladies to nearby Cobb's Pond? Just to kill time."

I went and grabbed Evan, and we nudged Ted to join us as well. I grabbed my video camera.

The other two women on the walk were Glennis Rasmussen and Liz Tanner, sisters-in-law from Minnesota. They were also returning home from a European vacation. We walked along the beautiful pond trail until we saw an area with benches, where we all sat and talked.

Evan entertained the group with our story about how this was the second time we were stuck without our suitcases on this trip. The first stop on our vacation was Nice, France. We flew there via Paris and somehow our luggage didn't make the connection. We were told by Air France they would send the luggage to our hotel when it arrived. We expected that to be a few hours, but it was more like a day and a half.

"They gave us a toothbrush, but after a day, we needed new clothes. So we went to a local grocery store called 'Monoprix,' where we each bought underwear, socks, and a cheap tourist T-shirt. We looked like we robbed a Goodwill box!" he said to roars of laughter.

Soon we were comparing stories about the amazing generosity we'd received. Sue said, "I came down for breakfast, and I was shocked that the volunteers at the college had made French toast and bacon. Someone rudely asked, 'Don't you have any scrambled eggs?' I couldn't believe it. I thought we'd be fortunate to have doughnuts and hot dogs. Maureen told the guy—these people are giving their all here, and you're asking for eggs? You're lucky we are not living on Cheez Doodles from the Mini-Mart. This place has a culinary school. It's been constant food like you'd see on a cruise. I think we gained ten pounds."

Like others, Sue and Maureen witnessed Gander's on-demand transportation system. "We were walking up to the corner store when a car stopped," said Sue. "He offered us a ride and we said, 'No thanks.' Then a second car pulled up. Same thing. It happened three times!"

Ted chimed in with a similar story. "I was just taking a walk down the street when a car pulled over. I thought, 'Have I done something wrong?' The driver wanted to know if I needed a ride anywhere and I had to say, 'I'm just trying to take a *walk* around your lovely town!'" We all laughed.

The air was getting chilly, so we all agreed to return to the college. Soon after arriving, we got the word from Mac that buses were on the way to the college to take us to the airport. Hallelujah, I thought.

As we were leaving, the college staff provided a final moment of kindness. They had packed to-go bags of snacks and fruit. They guessed correctly that our plane wouldn't be restocked with provisions for another flight. As we picked up our food, the staff lined the driveway to say good-bye.

I'll never forget one woman who cried, "Don't go!" I wasn't sure if this was because she was worried about our safety, or if she really enjoyed the companionship of 250 new friends.

CHAPTER 5

September 14th: Déjà Vu—Back in France

After Evan and I arrived at the airport, we checked in at the counter and confirmed that our destination was New York. The screening of carry-on bags seemed to take forever, as brand-new regulations meant you couldn't have any liquids or anything sharp like tweezers and razors.

After we passed through security, the gate agent informed us that, in fact, our plane was flying back to Paris. President Bush decided to only reopen US airspace to American airplanes, and Air France wanted their jet back. I remembered what Mac told me about ways to get back to America without taking a plane. I asked the gate agent, what if I don't want to go to Paris, if I want to take the bus and ferry? She said we could not do this now. We were *required* to stay inside the secured area. Our airline captain tried to dissuade those who wanted to travel to America by land and sea, because a hurricane was coming and he understood there were only two ferries available to cross the ocean from Newfoundland to Nova Scotia. He said, "Newfoundland took care of you up to now, but if you walk out the door, you are on your own."

Inside the international departures lounge, I went again to the pay phone and made two collect calls. I didn't remember being in a situation like this where I didn't like either one of my options. I called back to the office. Back in the Austin conference room, the staff took a vote. It was unanimous: Don't go back to Europe. Two staff members generously volunteered to drive thirty-six hours from Austin to the US-Canadian border in Maine to pick us up and drive us home (if the border was open). This seemed safe, but it would be an agonizing journey for everyone.

My next call was to my parents, where Mom immediately answered. I told her the situation, that essentially we had been lied to by the airline about our next destination.

"Don't get on the plane!" Mom cried.

I hung up, not sure what to do. I hated to disobey my mother's orders, but in my mind I was trying to project which course home would be the less stressful for both of us. I wasn't sure Evan could make the long journey by bus and ferry. My primary fear was being stuck in Europe for an extended period when I needed to get back to work at the office. I could hear the voices in my head of friends back home, saying, "Oh, poor you, stranded in Paris!"

Fourteen other passengers refused to board the plane once they learned the flight was heading back to Paris. They were content with abandoning their luggage for good. A security guard at the airport helped them charter a bus for $1,500 apiece. The bus would pick them up at 7:30 the next morning to take them to the US-Canadian border. They made a return trip to the College of the North Atlantic for one more night.

Evan wanted me to make the decision.

I knew that if we stuck with the airline, they would be obligated to get us to our final destination, with our bags full of clothes and European trinkets intact. If we decided to try a different route, it would be exhausting for everyone, expensive, and we would never get our possessions again. So, we stayed with Air France.

At least another hour went by before we could board. As we left the terminal and walked onto the tarmac, it was cold and dark. I could see our plane with the engines running. That was a good sign.

But instead of going to the plane, we were first directed to a school bus. Nobody told us why. After the bus was loaded, we drove across the runway with a police escort, lights flashing. I was mentally exhausted, hoping I had made the right choice. Evan turned the video camera on me and captured me with my head buried in my arm, resting on the seat in front of me. The bus stopped at a giant airplane hangar. Inside were thousands of pieces of luggage. We were told to go to a certain area, identify our own luggage, and gather it so that it could be retagged and loaded onto the plane. It took another hour or more for everyone to identify their bags and board. I was nervous that I had made the wrong decision. In a matter of hours, I went from feeling relaxed, sitting at Cobb's Pond talking to strangers, to being upset and anxious.

Ultimately, we took off into the night, eastbound over the Atlantic Ocean, flying back to Europe.

. . .

When we landed, it was morning in Paris. We were told to enter the terminal, and that we would receive a voucher for a hotel near the airport. No information was given about rebooking our flights.

"Come back to the airport in a couple days," an Air France representative told everyone.

After receiving our voucher, we entered the main terminal. As we walked in, we saw that every single person was standing frozen and quiet. It took a while to realize that thousands of people in a foreign country were having a moment of silence for the victims of the attacks in our country. They played the "Star-Spangled Banner" on TV and over the airport's public address system.

It wasn't just the airport that stood still. People all across Europe's highway systems stopped their vehicles and got out to stand at attention for this peaceful show of love for America.

It was truly moving, and I'll never forget it. I wondered if we, as Americans would ever do the same gesture for citizens of a foreign country. America has great respect in the world as a superpower. We help other countries when they have a crisis. Now it was our turn to deal with terrorism, and the rest of the world wanted to pay respect to America.

As soon as the moment ended, the airport erupted in chaos. There were thousands of stranded passengers inside and outside the terminal. Surprisingly, we got our luggage without any problems. That's when we said good-bye to Sue and Maureen. They would try to get the next flight back to Newark. They spent the night in a fleabag hotel Air France paid for, then returned to Charles de Galle Airport at 5 a.m. After much confusion they were given "refugee status" with bright orange tickets. They were put on a Continental Airlines flight that departed at 7:30 p.m. and landed in Newark at 11 p.m. Stepping into the terminal, Sue, Maureen, Liz, and Glennis got into a huddle and kissed Newark Airport floor even though it was dirty.

We wanted to stay completely away from the New York area, so we were put on a wait list for a flight direct from Paris to Houston on Continental Airlines. It's just an hour flight from there to home in Austin. We also said good-bye to our new friend Ted. He wasn't going back to New York; he was going back home to his flat in Paris. He offered to let us come and stay with him, but we also thought it would be easier to get back to the airport for a standby ticket if we stayed nearby.

As I walked out of the airport, I silently said the Lord's prayer. Somehow we found a shuttle to the Hotel Ibis, which was near the airport. It was a two-star hotel, and that was being generous with the stars. We checked in mid-afternoon, and even though it was a tiny, dirty hotel room, Evan crawled into bed, feeling sick. At least they had a small cable TV with the English news from BBC playing live coverage from America. I wasn't going to stay holed up there watching the planes hit the building for the twentieth time.

The hotel had a working telephone, so I called Sara back at my office and asked her to do the phone tree update saying that Evan and I were safe, back in the land where we started our journey home. I decided to take the train to downtown Paris to wander around.

When I arrived downtown, it felt different than just one week before, on what I thought was our last day in Europe. This time it was subdued on the streets. A digital sign on the Champs-Élysées read "Americans who need assistance should contact the US Embassy."

I spotted Notre Dame Cathedral. I needed to pray. As I walked there, I began singing in my head the "Peace Prayer." It was the Prayer of St. Francis: "Lord, make me an instrument of thy peace." Evan and I had sung this beautiful song one month before, at a concert for a civic choir in Austin. Growing up as a Catholic, I had sung another, more popular version from 1967, "Make Me a Channel of Your Peace," written by Sebastian Temple, based on the Prayer of St. Francis. With the hatred of this terrorist attack, the lyrics resonated deeply in my heart, especially "Where there is hatred, let me bring your love; where there is injury, your pardon, Lord; and where there's doubt, true faith in you," and "It is in pardoning that we are pardoned; in giving to all people, we receive; and in dying that we're born to eternal life."

Some might say it was too soon to look for joy, much less forgiveness. My faith was telling me that even in this darkest hour, I should be a witness for good. I certainly saw good all about me in Gander.

I went to a packed afternoon Mass at Notre Dame Cathedral, all spoken in French. I don't speak French, but I knew enough to know they were praying for their friends in *États-Unis* (the United States).

. . .

Over the next twenty-four hours, we both stayed in bed, watching news coverage from America and eating from the hotel restaurant. Attempts to reach the airline by phone were futile. But on Sunday, September 17th, we made a plan. We didn't want to haul all our bags to the airport if we weren't going to get a ticket that day. So, I took a few bags and headed over to the airport. I told Evan that if he didn't hear from me after a few hours, he should bring the rest of the luggage and come to the airport as well.

There were thousands of people waiting in enormous lines at every check-in counter. I moved a few inches each hour. I decided that I wasn't going to wait in a giant line only to be told to go home again. Most of the people in line had been on flights to America on September 12th, 13th, and 14th. Surely, I thought, our September 11th flight would have priority. The only problem was talking to someone from the airline. So I did the unthinkable.

I cut in line, in front of hundreds of people.

One woman busted me doing it. "Are you cutting in line?" she said.

"Look, I was on a flight that left here on September 11th, and we got diverted to this other country for days, and then they flew us back here!"

She nodded, and let me cut in front of her. This allowed me to merely get to the desk, and confirm that we were on an enormous standby list.

Evan showed up at the airport as planned. "Why didn't you call me?" he asked.

"I had no way to get out of this long line and find a pay

phone," I said. "Besides, I still have no idea if we will get a ticket home for today."

When we finally talked to the reservations agent at the desk, I decided that we wouldn't deal with Air France anymore. Continental had rushed an extra plane to Paris to help with the backlog of stranded passengers, so we hoped we would get on their direct flight to Houston. We were sent to another enormous line, where we were told that the airline would be holding a lottery for standby tickets.

"A lottery?! We've been trying to get home since the 11th," Evan said.

There were hundreds of anxious people waiting in a noisy terminal, and the two employees at the desk conducting the lottery didn't have a PA system to broadcast the names of the winners. They didn't know how to speak loudly, either. They called out the first name, "Smith, Ted Smith, party of four."

The ticket agents looked around, but didn't see Mr. Smith, who was fifty feet away. So they called another name, convinced Mr. Smith was a no-show.

"Wait!" Mr. Smith yelled, and he grabbed his bags, wife, and kids and squeezed his way past the other passengers to reach the counter.

He got his tickets, and the crowd cheered for him! The next name was called, and hardly anyone could hear the name. The crowd was getting angry. Did they call our name? People shouted, "Speak louder! We can't hear back here!"

Eventually the crowd devised its own communication system. Someone near the desk would hear the name called. This time it was "Sanchez, party of six." They would then turn around and yell, "Sanchez, party of six!" Twenty feet back, another person would hear it, and then turn around to the others behind him, and keep repeating the name until someone raised a hand and ran toward the front. It was like getting your name called on *The Price Is Right* game show. Come on down!

Names kept getting called, and none of them were ours. Evan and I were getting depressed; we just wanted to be home in Austin. I said another silent prayer that our names would be called. Finally, another airline employee came over. He had a louder voice. He yelled, "Tuerff, party of two!"

"HERE!" I screamed. "I'm coming, we're here!"

I raced to the front and was handed two boarding passes. I later told my father it felt like we were getting called up for a ticket into heaven.

Security was tighter than ever, but when we finally boarded our plane and it took off, we breathed a little easier.

. . .

When we finally made it home, we took two days off to recuperate. When Evan and I returned to the office, we walked into the conference room and everyone was waiting for a surprise welcome-home celebration.

Everyone was wearing a red French beret, and many had penciled in mustaches on their lips. They had beignets and champagne to celebrate our return. There was a giant "Welcome home" banner, which had been signed by the entire staff.

I was moved by what my colleagues had done for me, but by this time I had begun to see stories of compassion and kindness from all over the world. People had been holding candlelight prayer vigils on every continent. Thousands of first responders and average citizens drove cross-country to volunteer at the World Trade Center's "Ground Zero." Cabbies in New York City stopped honking their horns in traffic. Long lines were seen at local blood banks.

Tributes were held across the world. Even political enemies united in grief, hope, and solidarity.

After a few weeks, I wrote an email summary of our experience in Gander to share with my staff, family, and friends. The *Austin Business Journal* got hold of the email and a reporter wrote "An Exec's Newfound Grit." It was the first story about Gander's kindness to strangers. It appeared on September 30, 2001.

In November 2001, I got a call from Maureen in New Jersey that they had given my name to a producer at ABC News who had read a newspaper story about Gander. He was looking for video footage, and they remembered I had shot video while we were together. An hour later, I took a call from David Perozzi, a producer for ABC's *PrimeTime Live* show. He asked me about my experience in Gander and then asked me if I could send him the footage. He also asked if I would be willing to fly to New York for an in-studio interview for the show. At that time, many people were still afraid to fly, worried that more airplanes might be hijacked. I agreed to fly, and I brought Evan along for the trip to Manhattan so we could go see a Broadway show.

Sue Riccardelli had already been interviewed for the segment, but Maureen and Sue took the train into Manhattan to meet us for a fun reunion dinner. We all agreed that we'd been lucky to wind up at the College of the North Atlantic under the leadership of Mac Moss. We also believed it truly was remarkable what everyone in this tiny town had done, and we weren't sure the same volunteer response would have happened in rural America.

When it was time for my interview with reporter Jay Schadler, a fancy Lincoln Town Car came to pick me up, and I insisted that Evan come with me. I had done plenty of TV interviews in my career, but I was nervous about coming up with a good sound bite to accurately describe our time in Gander.

"You'll be fine," Evan assured me. "Maybe you could say, 'On that tragic day, the people of Gander restored my faith in humanity.'" I loved it, because it was authentic.

David Perozzi was very kind, giving us a personal tour of ABC News headquarters. Just one month prior, ABC had received a package of anthrax in the mail. That had started another US terror scare involving offices around the East Coast. The anthrax killed five and put seventeen others in the hospital. Perozzi pointed out the "thrax" elevator that had carried the mail. He tried to avoid riding that specific elevator, but he didn't seem afraid of working in the building.

The ABC story, called "Angels of Hope," aired in December 2001. We held a watching party for staff and friends at my office late that night. When they saw my face on the screen, everyone cheered. They used the video clip of the Eiffel Tower, with me narrating, "Here we are walking up to the Eiffel Tower, on September 10th, I believe." It felt odd to celebrate my national TV debut because it was related to 9/11, but I felt comforted knowing that Americans could see and hear the story of light amid the darkness, via Newfoundland.

The reporter interviewed one of the Gander school bus drivers who broke their picket line to help with transportation.

When asked why, he said, "We believe in doing good deeds for good people, especially the Americans."

Perhaps his sound bite about good deeds would be my inspiration for what to do on the first anniversary of 9/11.

CHAPTER 6

One Year Later—Pay It Forward 9/11

When we left Gander, the volunteers said our gratitude was enough and repayment for the food or phone calls wasn't necessary. Their generosity provided a beautiful example of how little things can make a big difference.

Like many people, I was changed by 9/11. However, I didn't succumb to fear of new terrorist attacks, perhaps because of the blessing I witnessed in Gander. My religious faith was rekindled as a result of the experience. I soon started attending weekly Mass again. Even though I moved farther away, outside central Austin, I decided to stick with the University Catholic Center, my parish home that had helped me during my time of need in the early 1990s. I always felt welcome there. My prayer life was focused on peace.

On the first anniversary of the attacks, in 2002, I wanted to go back to Gander, as some come from aways did. But the cost and time for me to travel from Austin to Gander would have been greater than a round-trip airfare to Paris.

I wanted to do something to offer my gratitude, but what? Sitting at my office desk, an idea hit me. I borrowed an idea from the book and movie *Pay It Forward* by Catherine Ryan Hyde. This touching fictional work demonstrated how a young boy could start a movement that promoted kindness to strangers. I wondered if there was a way to use that concept to demonstrate my gratitude for Gander. The country was still anxious and angry about 9/11, but perhaps we could give people hope.

We divided staff into teams of two and helped them with their kindness assignment by giving each a hundred-dollar bill. PHOTO CREDIT: SARA BEECHNER

As a co-owner of a small business with twenty-five employees, I decided to try mandating participation by the staff in doing good deeds for strangers. We would make it fun by breaking the staff into teams of two and giving each team a hundred-dollar bill. These teams could then use the hundred dollars for any act of kindness to strangers. Unsure whether staff would go along with this, I ran the idea by a couple of longtime employees. They wholeheartedly approved. The staff vividly remembered being at the office on 9/11 and the added stress of making sure their bosses were safe.

We closed the office the morning of September 11, 2002, to allow time for the teams to do their work. Staff members were instructed to anonymously perform random acts of kindness. But, they were also told to try to explain the story of what had happened to their boss in Gander on 9/11. At the end of the day, we gathered in a conference room and each team explained how they had spent their money. People got teary-eyed as they talked about the amazing reactions they received when they did small things like buying coffee or giving away bus passes to a stranger. There was something magical when they made that one-on-one connection, just as I experienced when the teenager gave me the air mattress and pillows on 9/11 in Gander.

The first year, two teams of staff remarkably ran into each other at the local charity hospital in Austin. Both had the same idea to visit the maternity ward to support a new mother who was giving birth to a baby that day. The nurses at the hospital told both teams that there were two single mothers who had given birth that day. Both mothers were certain to need the money.

One team purchased a hundred-dollar savings bond and wrote a card stating: "Because your baby is born on a day that will always be linked to a day of tragedy, we'd like you to have something positive you may share with the child in future years." The other team gave a card and their hundred-dollar bill.

Another team gave their hundred dollars to the owner of a breakfast diner, telling him to use the money to pay for the next several checks until the money ran out, probably after about eight tabs. He promised to remind customers that it was the anniversary of 9/11 and encourage them to pay it forward by doing a good deed for a stranger that day.

Another team decided to break the hundred-dollar bill into a hundred singles. They paper-clipped a note to each one explaining Pay It Forward 9/11. They went to a busy street corner in Austin and tried to hand the dollars randomly to people in their cars at the stoplight. To their surprise, it was extremely difficult to get most people to roll down their window to accept the gift. "What's the catch?" people kept asking over and over.

Being in the marketing business, we weren't surprised to find people skeptical of an offer of free money. Others gave an appreciative smile, or choked back tears, mentioning they knew someone who died that day. Emergency first responders were always on someone's kindness list. One team spent their cash buying several tubs of ice cream and delivering them to local fire stations.

One year later, the word got out to the *Austin American-Statesman* newspaper, and reporter Andrea Ball hunted down someone who had received a gift the first year. She wrote: "One team gave $100 to the founder of Comfort House, which provides food, day care, and emotional support to children in a low-income neighborhood. 'Spend it on yourself,' they told her. She didn't. She spent it on the Comfort House food bank, buying enough supplies to feed fifty seniors for a month. She said, 'It did so much for us. I figured angels just gave me a gift.'"

Ball even tracked down Gander mayor Claude Elliott for the story. He said of the Gander 9/11 response, "We did the only thing we know how to do, which was to comfort them, console them, and show them some love."

The newspaper article blew my company's anonymous cover. I received an emotional voice mail on my office phone that made that okay. The caller said, "Hello, Kevin, you don't know me. My name is Vincent. I just wanted to thank you. This morning I had a flat tire. I took it to get fixed and one of your employees paid for it. At first, I was kind of puzzled about the whole thing, until just now at 3:00, I'm reading the front page of the newspaper. The article starts out, 'Something special could happen to you today.' And it did. I had no idea that any of this had occurred to anybody in Austin. But, I want to thank you very much. It was very heartfelt. What you're doing is very kind, and you *really* made a difference in my life. I just wanted to thank you."

That difference cost exactly $7. Seven others with flat tires received the service for free that day. I got choked up listening to the voice mail. I thought, *Maybe this is an example of what Luke's Gospel in the Bible was encouraging, "Do unto others as you would have them do unto you."*

I told Ball in the article, "Everybody's lives are so frantic and busy. Often it takes a jump start to remind us of the importance of being kind to strangers. It doesn't take a whole lot of effort to make an impact."

. . .

A woman in Austin, not connected to the company, heard about the idea that morning and immediately decided to start baking. She and her husband lived in the New York City area for many years, and some of their neighbors were killed in the World Trade Center.

She and her husband read about Pay It Forward 9/11 in the newspaper. After reading the article, they looked at each other, headed for the big chest freezer in the garage, grabbed the home-baked cookies that could always be found there, and began placing them on baking trays. After hours of baking, they packaged the cookies into plastic sandwich bags, two cookies per bag, and tied each bag with a red, white, and blue ribbon, with a note saying, "Please do an act of kindness today in memory of those victims of 9/11."

Then the woman and her husband ran out the front door and began hopping on neighborhood school buses. They gave the cookies away, explaining that the cookies were sort of "free"—the only payment required was that the kids would promise to do an act of kindness. The bus drivers offered to take those cookies left over to the school offices and for the staff. Everyone wanted to be included in what felt right and good to be doing.

She liked doing this so much that she called and left me a voice message. "Kevin, you don't know me but my name is Kitten, and I think this Pay It Forward idea to remember September 11th is fantastic."

She went on to describe what she did. A month later, I was in Washington, DC, for work and I saw a college friend named John Howard, Jr., an appointee of President George W.

Bush, at a conference. He said, "Hey, I heard about that Pay It Forward program. That was really cool."

I thanked him and told him about my voice message from the lady who made cookies. He asked, "Do you remember who she was?"

I said, "Sure, it was a funny name, like 'Kitten.'"

John started laughing hard, saying, "That's my mom! What a small world—right?"

Kitten and her husband, John Howard, Sr., would become two of the effort's greatest supporters, baking cookies for school kids every 9/11 for ten years. What they didn't expect was how many people in the Austin area had a connection to the attacks in Washington, DC, and New York City. An office worker at one of the elementary schools said she counted on those cookies every anniversary of 9/11 because her brother died in the towers and it hurt her so much that some Americans didn't even know what 9/11 was.

"What we started in 2002 grew in joyful ways to our extended family, neighbors, several school districts, churches, and Girl and Boy Scouts," Kitten later told me. "Everyone wanted to be a part of the progress of America's coming together, day-by-day, week-by week, and year-by-year. Everyone loved their role in helping the healing."

. . .

In 2003, our company, which focused on doing good in the world, experienced a horrible betrayal that brought our company to its knees. It was a time filled with stress, anxiety, and paranoia. We needed an emergency infusion of cash to stay afloat. Sadly, our bank and many others wouldn't help us when we really needed money to bridge a cash flow gap. Thanks to my family, we secured a loan and then paid it off in less than a year.

That September, when it was time for the anniversary of 9/11, we had every reason to stop continuing our tradition. Instead, our hardworking staff pulled the company through the crisis. They really loved the Pay It Forward 9/11 initiative, so we kept it alive. We could've continued without the charitable expense of a hundred dollars per team, but it felt right to continue just as we always had, with the hundred-dollar bills. Many prayers were answered that year. Good prevailed over evil, as our company continued to prosper for years to come. Where there was despair, we kept hope.

By 2006, friends, family, and several businesses had joined in our initiative from Texas and other states. A local law firm joined in. Two of their employees distributed two hundred dollars by purchasing gas for strangers. They waited at the pump and surprised the drivers as they prepared to pay. Also that year, one EnviroMedia team gave twenty-five-dollar gift cards to four shoppers at a grocery store in a low-income neighborhood. Others handed out water and Gatorade to construction workers at a downtown site. Everyone felt they made a connection with other humans they hadn't experienced before. The staff considered this day the highlight of their year working at the company.

CHAPTER 7

Ten Years Later—The Return to Gander

By the tenth anniversary of 9/11, people were starting to treat the anniversary as just another day of the year. Since "Never forget" was the mantra of our country after the attacks, my company decided to use our marketing skills to renew the idea of remembering the tragic day by doing even more good deeds or community service on its anniversary. We donated cash and pro bono services to the California-based Pay It Forward Foundation to support their great idea we'd been implementing for ten years. I was able to talk by phone with the book and movie's author, Catherine Ryan Hyde. She appreciated what we were doing and through a YouTube video personally encouraged her foundation's supporters to join the tenth-anniversary effort with good deeds for strangers.

Throughout this time, I had been corresponding with friends in Gander. After ten years of giving thanks to Gander through my initiative, it was time for me to return to Gander to finally say thanks in person.

EnviroMedia had grown in staff size to support thirty teams of two for the Pay It Forward 9/11 initiative in Austin as well as in Portland, Oregon, and Seattle, Washington. I would be bringing to Gander a $1,000 charitable donation to the College of the North Atlantic to help continue the Air France 004 passenger scholarship for students who are recognized for helping others.

Evan and I had unfortunately ended our relationship, so he wouldn't be making the reunion trip with me. Instead, I was joined by Melanie Fish, a friend and manager who worked at my company.

These days, it's still not easy to fly to Gander, even from New York airports. We started our journey to Newfoundland with a visit to the national 9/11 memorial in New York City. The names of those who died in the terrorist attacks are inscribed in bronze around the twin memorial pools. Melanie and I felt the deep sadness of the tragedy. We didn't speak much as we walked around the memorial at Ground Zero. Before leaving, I donated $100 for a cobblestone at the memorial plaza in honor of the people of Gander, Newfoundland.

The next day, we flew on Air Canada from Newark to Halifax to catch a connecting flight to Gander on a small regional jet. Alas, we were met with delays due to bad weather at Newark Airport. We sat on the tarmac for hours before we took off. Later, when we landed at our connection, we could see the plane for Gander at another gate, so we hoped we wouldn't miss the connecting flight. We rushed to Canadian customs, but it took too long, and our flight left without us. I was stranded in Canada once again. By this time it was 1 a.m., and the next flight to Gander would be another connecting flight through St. John's, Newfoundland, at 6 a.m. The next nonstop to Gander was much later in the day. The Halifax Airport was deserted. Rather than sleep in the airport, we found a nearby hotel with two rooms available, deciding that four hours of sleep in a bed was better.

Everything happens for a reason. If we hadn't missed that connecting direct flight, we wouldn't have met a special man from Gander on the connecting flight from St. John's to Gander. It was a small twelve-seater jet, much smaller than the 747 I flew on in 2001. When I started snapping photos out the window, a gentleman in front of me turned around and asked us where we were from. I explained that I was returning for the first time for a 9/11 passenger reunion. Melanie described what our company had been doing with Pay It Forward each year. Apparently, that moved him to do his own good deed.

"Would ya like to take a flight around the Gander area while you're in town?" he said with his thick Newfie accent. "Ya see, I own this plane, and I also own the flight school in Gander. We just got a brand-new four-seater Cessna plane. If you'd like, I'll have one of my pilots take you up for a spin on Sunday."

Of course we accepted this gracious offer. I asked if we might fly up to the North Atlantic to see the melting glaciers from Greenland that are floating south. As someone concerned about climate change and melting glaciers, I was excited.

When we landed at the Gander Airport, the other passengers deplaned and we stayed behind for a few minutes.

Melanie turned on our video camera and recorded me giving a few thoughts about being back in Gander since the chaos ten years prior.

"Almost ten years to the day, I'm back in Gander, Newfoundland. I was stranded here on 9/11 when our plane was diverted here. I'm on a much smaller, tiny plane right now. Back then, I was on the second of thirty-eight aircraft that were brought here to this small, tiny town. I'm excited to be back, and see some of the folks to reunite from 9/11."

Mac Moss personally greeted me at Gander International Airport, ten years after I was diverted there on 9/11. PHOTO CREDIT: KEVIN TUERFF

When I finally walked inside the terminal, there was Mac Moss, my 9/11 hero. The place looked a lot different from the time Evan and I rolled in, tired after our long nightmare on

Air France. In 2001, there were hundreds of volunteers there with tables and free food. This time, there were about a dozen workers inside the airport.

A reporter from CBC-TV (national Canadian network) was there to catch our airport reunion. He interviewed me and had me recount my memories about the place. Throughout the reunion weekend, I did several interviews with local, national, and international TV and radio reporters, and I did a live call-in interview at a local radio station. In true Gander fashion, Mac invited a newspaper reporter and photographer from Toronto back to his home for a cookout, which was photographed for the national *Globe and Mail*.

After years of telling this story, it never gets old for me. And still, I find that so many people have no idea about the generosity that Gander showed us that day. Humans need good role models, and the folks in Gander are just that. I truly felt blessed to be a come from away, so I could spread the good news of hope for humanity, even in our darkest hours.

Once we checked into our hotel, I was ecstatic to see Maureen and Sue there in the lobby. We had corresponded often, but this was the first time I'd seen them since 2001. They've been visiting Gander on their summer vacation every other year since 2001.

Sue, Maureen, and I joined Mac and others for a special assembly with all the students of the College of the North Atlantic–Gander campus. It was my first time back at the college, and it was strange to see students everywhere instead of haggard airline passengers, cupcakes, and sleeping bags.

Gratitude in Gander: I joined other come from aways to serve breakfast to 9/11 volunteers like Nellie Moss and Sue Walsh. PHOTO CREDIT: KEVIN TUERFF

The next morning, the Lions Club held a community breakfast at the hockey rink (a place Mayor Elliott called the "world's largest refrigerator" years earlier, when all the donated food for stranded passengers needed a place to be kept at a safe temperature). All plane people who had returned for the reunion were invited to be servers on the buffet line. It was rewarding to be able to dish out scrambled eggs to people who had volunteered for Americans and other foreigners ten years ago. It was my way to finally show my thanks, person-to-person.

The commemorative events in Gander that I was a part of exceeded what most American cities (especially small towns) were doing to mark the 9/11 tenth anniversary. Perhaps Americans still didn't see anything good to celebrate. For America, the anniversary is a day of mourning. In Gander, it is a reminder of how they helped the world.

The reunion with the plane people was a cause for celebration, including a benefit concert at the hockey rink with the Navigators, a Newfoundland rock band. After arriving at the concert, Mayor Elliott asked me to speak to the packed crowd about my experiences in Gander. Other speakers included representatives of Lufthansa Airlines, who donated a big check to the mayor. I wasn't nervous at all. I felt at home. I knew I was safe with the loving people of Gander.

"Hello, Gander!" I said, and the crowd cheered. "I was a passenger on the second plane that landed here ten years ago, and I experienced the amazing generosity of your kindness then. As one of many Americans who were here, I say thank you for giving me food, clothing, and shelter. I was at the College of the North Atlantic, and everyone we met there was fantastic! So, thank you to everyone who volunteered."

I went on, "Every year on the anniversary of 9/11 at my company in Austin, we tell the story of Gander. We send out teams of our staff into the community and I give my employees a hundred dollars to use for doing good deeds for strangers and telling them about what happened here on 9/11."

I looked to Mayor Elliott. This was my first time to meet the mayor face-to-face, and we wouldn't see each other again until opening night of *Come From Away* at Ford's Theatre in Washington, DC, in 2016. "So, Mr. Mayor, I don't have a check for you, but I have a request. I want you in Gander to help me spread 10,000 good deeds across the world. We can prove that through darkness there is light, starting here in Canada. We can prove that we can all make a difference, one good deed at a time."

Next thing I knew, I was out dancing to a jig on the dance

floor by myself and several local ladies came up to dance with me. It was a blast.

. . .

On Sunday morning (September 11th), Melanie and I had arranged to take our free flight over Newfoundland, in a brand-new Cessna twin-engine airplane. This airplane was so new it had "new car smell" from the upholstered leather seats.

We met our young pilot at the flight school. Melanie allowed me to sit in the copilot seat (I secretly wanted to learn how to fly a plane) while she sat behind me. The plane had high-tech navigation devices that made flying as simple as using a joystick. We put our headphones on and taxied the empty jetway to the runway at YQX. No jumbo jets today— just us, cleared for takeoff.

The pilot had been told to take us for a spin around Gander. When I asked if we could see the glaciers near Fogo Island, about an hour-long round-trip, he said sure. We flew over the beautiful forests that cover most of Newfoundland until we reached the blue waters of the North Atlantic. Our pilot pointed out several chunks of glaciers. Being a climate change geek, I asked if we could go low enough for me to snap some photos. He did.

Mac Moss, who sails the ocean frequently, told us floating glaciers weren't unusual, but having big ones float south in September was definitely unusual. It was evidence of climate change that I'd only read about in research papers and news reports.

After seeing the glaciers, we set a course for YQX again.

After a while, the pilot talked on his headset to Melanie and me. "Would you like to fly?" he asked.

Melanie almost passed out because she knew I would say yes. The pilot explained the basics of how to hold the steering wheel, flipped a few switches, and that was it: I was flying! He told me I should follow the navigation arrows on the computer screen, and not just turn the steering wheel willy-nilly. The slightest movement in your hands would turn the aircraft off course.

All in all, I didn't fly that many minutes, but it was one of the coolest things I've ever done. The pilot landed us safely back in Gander about fifteen minutes later.

Funny thing about the pilot: One week later, when Melanie and I were reviewing pictures of the Gander benefit concert, I noticed a familiar guy dancing behind me in one photo while I was on the dance floor. I emailed our pilot a copy of the photo. "Thanks again for the wonderful airplane ride over Newfoundland. By chance are you the guy dancing behind me in this photo?" I wrote.

"Guilty as charged," he replied.

. . .

Mac and Nellie invited me, Melanie, Sue, and Maureen to their house for dinner with their neighbors who live on Little Cobb's Pond. It's a quiet, lovely place with beautiful trees lining the pond.

After dinner, we were surprised to hear a giant ruckus in the house. Maureen, Sue, and Mac came around the corner wearing bright yellow raincoats and hats. One was banging on an "ugly stick," a traditional Newfoundland musical instrument made out of a mop handle with bottle caps and small bells. They informed us we were about to be named honorary Newfoundlanders, in a process called "the screech-in."

After eating some salty dried fish, they gave Melanie and me a shot of screech (or rum) as part of the ceremony.

"Are ye a screecher?" Mac asked.

Sue and Maureen were screeched in years before. They told us to respond, "'Deed I is, me ol' cock! And long may yer big jib draw!" It's a tongue twister. Translated, it means "Yes, I am, my old friend, and may your sails always catch wind."

With the kiss of a Newfoundland codfish, I was screeched into being an honorary Newfoundlander. PHOTO CREDIT: KEVIN TUERFF

After drinking the shot and eating a piece of Newfoundland steak (baloney meat), Mac anointed us by placing the oars of a rowing paddle on each shoulder. Then it was time to kiss a fish, a Newfoundland cod. Lucky for us, the fish was frozen. We both kissed the fish, making it official. We even received an official certificate announcing our honorary citizenship.

Fourteen years after we started Pay It Forward 9/11, Melanie's husband Dan told me how joining the effort had changed him for the better. He said, "We started over five years ago when our daughters brought small gifts to firefighters. It had such a big impact on everyone. We participate every year on the 9/11 anniversary. Now I find myself doing random good deeds more often. I recently helped a stranded motorist who ran out of gas this past summer. He had walked a half mile from his car to a gas station in hundred-degree heat. I pulled up and asked him if he wanted a ride back to his car. He was suspicious of me; I was a big guy and a stranger. I know that my actions made an impact. I got that idea from you and Melanie."

"If a bunch of international planes landed near the small town of Bastrop (Texas), I'd go out and pick up a family and bring them back home. I just wasn't exposed to this before."

In 2014, my 9/11 heroes Mac and Nellie emailed to say they were visiting Florida soon, so they wanted to swing by Texas and visit me. This was their first trip to the Lone Star State. These Gander folks set the bar of hospitality so high that I was anxious.

Showing some Texas hospitality to my Gander friends Nellie and Mac Moss at Austin Bergstrom International Airport in 2014. PHOTO CREDIT: KEVIN TUERFF

First up, I greeted them at the airport with a "Welcome to Texas" sign. I also bought them each a "Keep Austin Weird" T-shirt (the city's slogan). We posed for a photo near baggage claim after they landed. Because I lived in a one-bedroom apartment, I encouraged them to stay in a nearby hotel. I made them a care package with some snacks, bottled water, "Don't mess with Texas" shot glasses, and some Texas tequila. They loved it.

After they checked in, I took them out to dinner and gave them a brief driving tour of downtown Austin. We visited the eclectic shops of South Congress Avenue, a Western wear store, and the Lady Bird Johnson Wildflower Center. The multiyear drought was letting up, and recent rains delivered some beautiful flowers. We also visited Lake Travis and the famous Oasis restaurant with its terrific view of the lake and the Hill Country.

I brought the Mosses by EnviroMedia to meet some of the staff who participated in our annual kindness initiative. I organized a special staff meeting so they could meet Mac and Nellie. Many of them knew the story of Gander through their annual participation in Pay It Forward 9/11, but I wanted them to hear it again, from Gander's perspective. It was a casual conversation, with staff asking several questions about the town's response. Mac and Nellie were generous with their compliments on the work the company was doing to protect the environment, and they were thankful for our gratitude via Pay It Forward 9/11 in the name of Gander. That conversation was Nellie's favorite part of the visit.

In the summer of 2016, after nearly 20 years of starting and managing EnviroMedia as president, my business partner purchased my shares and I stepped down from the company. At age 50, it opened a new chapter in my life.

My new freedom allowed me to spend more time participating in events related to *Come From Away*.

In September 2016, the show was in production at Ford's Theater in Washington, DC, a city which suffered 184 deaths of workers at the Pentagon and the souls flying on American Airlines Flight 77 fifteen years prior.

The show's producers organized an entire performance for survivors and their family members of the attack on the Pentagon. Kathy Dillaber, a retired Department of Army civilian and long-time docent for the Pentagon 9/11 memorial attended the show. Kathy is a survivor, but lost her younger sister, Patty Dillaber Mickey, who worked in a nearby corridor of the Pentagon, just 50 yards away. She lost 24 workers in her office alone.

Kathy was so moved by the story of Gander, she invited me and others whose stories are portrayed in *Come From Away* to visit the Pentagon and the 9/11 Pentagon Memorial. Lisa, a representative from the DoD, arranged for our tour and escort into the Pentagon. We happened to arrive at the same time of an interior 9/11 remembrance, a closed ceremony for the Pentagon employees and their invited guests. We told Lisa that we would be honored if we could attend the ceremony, so she took us out to center court. It was a moving tribute from top military officials, with the playing of patriotic songs, including "Taps," by a marine musician.

Afterward, Kathy gave me, Beverley Bass, and Nick and Diane Marson a special behind-the-scenes tour of the Pentagon so we could better understand what happened on the 9/11 attack. We visited the 9/11 Memorial room and chapel and went to the outdoor 9/11 Pentagon memorial, located on the side building where the attack took place. It is a moving memorial park with 184 benches, one for each victim: 125 Pentagon workers, 59 passengers, and the flight crew on American Airline 77.

Despite having no staff to organize and participate in the annual Pay It Forward 9/11 in 2016, I wanted to carry on the tradition. I approached producer Sue Frost, and Marlene and Kenny Alhadeff, executive producers at Junkyard Dog Productions, the company producing *Come From Away*. They already knew the history of my annual tradition because it's mentioned in the show's script. I asked if the cast, band, and crew would like to join me on the 15th anniversary of the 9/11 attacks. Everyone quickly agreed to participate and a few days before the anniversary, we gathered everyone in the Lincoln board room at Ford's theater to explain how each team had $100 bills to use to do at least three good deeds. Kenny Alhadeff made a passionate speech about the power of kindness and handed out the $100 bills to participants.

I saw the show for a second time that week, including a matinee on the afternoon of September 11. I had the honor of delivering a post-show discussion that afternoon and 2/3 of the audience stayed after the final curtain. The theater said it was the best attended post-show discussion ever. I told the history of Pay It Forward 9/11 and a few cast members told their stories of how they spent their $100 on random acts of kindness. Rodney Hicks, who plays "Bob" and other characters, explained his own surprise after jumping in line to purchase someone's lunch at a fast food restaurant. "I didn't realize how we don't look at each other in the eyes like we used to." He said, "Perhaps that's because we're all so busy with our heads down, buried in the electronic devices that are meant to connect us together."

After the show, several of my friends and I went to a nearby Greek restaurant for dinner. To everyone's shock, when the bill arrived, the waiter told us it was paid for by someone unknown! Inside our bill holder was a piece of paper that read "Pay It Forward 9/11." Everyone thought I was the person who picked up the tab, but I wasn't. I'd been organizing and promoting random acts of kindness for this effort for years, but this was the first time my friends and I were recipients. We tried to guess who the benefactor was, but it's still a mystery.

In 2016, I was interviewed for a story about *Come From Away* for National Public Radio. Reporter Wade Goodwyn briefly explains my gratefulness and skepticism in the broadcast. He says, "As he flew away from Gander, Tuerff vowed to himself he was going to try to live his life like the honorary Ganderite he'd become."

Then came my voice:

"They don't think that they did anything special and that we would do this for anybody at any time. But I wondered, would we—in America, would we do what they did? And I wasn't sure."

CHAPTER 8

What Now? Kindness and Refugees

"For I was hungry and you gave me food, I was thirsty and you
gave me drink, I was a stranger and you welcomed me."

—Matthew, 25:35

On September 12th, 2016, after my plane departed Reagan
National airport, I was suddenly overwhelmed with emotion.
It felt like I was intoxicated, but I promise I wasn't drinking
Grey Goose vodka (or any alcohol). Thinking about the song,
"Prayer" from the musical, I pulled out my iPhone to listen
to the music, "Make Me a Channel of Your Peace." I did a
search for the word "peace" in iTunes and it turns out I had a
couple versions of the prayer of St. Francis, along with other
peace-related songs sung by Jackson Browne and Joan Arma-
trading. As I listened to these songs, I was brought to tears.
A friend had encouraged me to journal about the weekend's
activities. I opened my laptop and typed without thinking: "I
am embracing my role as a channel of peace."

After my flight landed, I felt a sense of joy, excitement, and bewilderment about what this in-flight experience really meant.

Two weeks later, I received an email from my dear friend who is now a practicing shaman in New Mexico. We'd been friends since college in the late 1980s. His email asked, "Who is that friend of yours who died when we were in our twenties?"

I was unsure why he was asking, but I replied that I sadly remembered about a dozen friends who died of AIDS during my twenties. I wrote back listing their names: Bill, Javier, David, Tom, Gary, and the others. My friend replied: "I sense Gary's spirit is with you and he's aware of what is going on in your life. Talk (pray) to him."

Okay, that's freaky, I thought. Yet, the more I thought about Gary, I remembered it was he who gave me the courage to leave my comfortable state government job to start EnviroMedia. You see, in 1996, Gary had recently left his salaried job for a 100 percent commission-based real estate sales job. I was debating about starting a company without any investors, and I was nervous. Gary and I met at Texas French Bread in South Austin for lunch one day. I asked him, "Gary, what are you going to do if you don't make sales and end up without a paycheck?"

He assured me he was confident he would make money. He then asked me, "Kevin, when have you ever worked your absolute hardest and failed?"

I thought for a moment, "I can't think of a single time."

Gary said, "Then start that company!"

A few months later, I left my job and started the company with my friend Valerie that would occupy most of my time for more than 19 years. Now it was wonderful to know that Gary was here with me in spirit, at a time when I was beginning my next life chapter after leaving EnviroMedia.

A few weeks later, I was visiting my parents in Nashville. A friend from college lived there for many years. We kept up with each other via Facebook, and four years prior we both suffered the loss of our mutual friend Alexis due to pancreatic cancer at age 54. My friend invited me to dinner so we could catch up. I learned that she was studying to become a Buddhist chaplain. Shortly after we sat down for dinner, I said, "I've been thinking about Alexis. Facebook Memories reminded me it's been four years since she passed."

She replied, "I've been thinking a lot about Alexis, too. In fact, I've been sensing messages from her. She wants me to give you a stack of letters she wrote to me in 1990."

She reached into her purse and pulled a stack of a dozen hand-written letters, written on yellow legal paper. The energy coming from those letters felt as if they were on fire.

I went to my parent's home and read them. I was sure I'd find something remarkable written in there, perhaps an idea for my next career. Nope. I was barely mentioned. I did take some notes from one letter, which she said, "I recently read a book about spirituality, and here's my takeaways . . . one that stood out was, 'Ask God for what you want.'"

After these three incidents, I called my good friend who is a Catholic priest. I told him about these three unusual encounters and asked him what I should make of all this. He said, "I think God is trying to talk to you. You should consider an 8-day spiritual retreat with the Jesuit Fathers to discern what it means."

If I had still been working full-time at my company, I would've never taken off work for an 8-day spiritual retreat. I looked online and found many options across the country. The first opening was at the Jesuit Center for Spiritual Growth in Wernersville, Pennsylvania. I read it was a *silent* retreat, but I thought that was optional. Wrong! No phone, no TV, no social media, no talking, even at meals in the cafeteria with 40 other retreat participants.

I began daily spiritual direction with a Jesuit brother, who taught me about Ignation contemplative prayer, or praying with imagination. I've always had a creative imagination. I used to pretend I was one of the paramedics on the 1970s TV show *Emergency!* I wandered the beautiful 400-acre grounds to meditate and pray. I reflected on certain Gospels, by imagining myself there, in the scene of the biblical story. After 45-minutes of meditating, I would journal what I saw, felt, or heard. I shared the unusual encounters I'd been having with my spiritual director. He asked me what notes I had taken from Alexis' letters. When I read off the list of bullets she wrote after reading a book on spirituality, his eyes got big when I mentioned, "Ask God for what you want."

He said, "You haven't studied Ignatian Spirituality yet, but this is one of the primary tenets."

Wow, I thought. Maybe Alexis wanted me to be at that spiritual retreat.

Midway through the week, I signed up to receive a massage from a local massage therapist who came to the center from the nearby town. I received a one-hour relaxing massage. I laid face down on the table, drifting in-and-out of sleep. A poster in the hallway read, "Pay attention to your daydreams as a way to talk with God." I liked that.

I remember the therapist rubbing my upper back and

shoulders in circles. Just then, I had a vision. There were letters appearing, as if written on a white board. They came in slowly, one at a time: *i-m-m-i-g-r-a-n-t*. What was that, I thought? *Immigrant.*

My mind was racing. I wanted to tell someone about this strange experience, especially since I'd never had a vision before. But it was a silent retreat, I had to wait until the next day to speak with my spiritual director. When I asked him what it meant he said, "I don't know, but you're going to pray about it to find the answer." My meditation and prayer wasn't providing immediate answers, so I went on a hike along a nearby creek, while listening to music on my headphones. With my iTunes randomly shuffling songs, I was surprised when the computer chose the beautiful music from the movie soundtrack, "A River Runs Through It." I repeatedly listened to the song, "Haunted by Waters." With extreme weather due to climate change, many countries are facing a crisis with too much water or not enough water, causing massive flooding and extended droughts.

At the end of my retreat, I was using contemplative prayer to ask Jesus for help. *Should I continue focusing my passion on environment, or should I switch to promoting kindness to strangers, immigrants and refugees?*

Within my meditative prayer, in my subconscious came two words: "Of course."

I interpreted that to mean of course I should switch my passion, either in advocacy or a career. After further meditation, I considered I may have a calling to use my environmental expertise to work for climate refugees. According to Refugees International, "each year millions of people are driven from their homes by floods, storms, droughts, or other weather-related disasters."

Months later, I was in New York City to bring my friend Todd, the friend in Amsterdam who I reached by phone on 9/11, to see *Come From Away*. I was encouraged to bring my book to the priest at St. Francis Xavier, a Jesuit parish in Manhattan. When the taxi pulled up, I opened the door and directly in my line of sight was a huge banner that read, "Welcome Immigrants and Refugees."

During Mass, I had another spiritual encounter. I felt like I was intoxicated again, though I was sober. In my prayer, I asked God, "Is this church supposed to be my spiritual home?"

And again, from my subconscious mind, I felt a very strong *YES!*

I'd always said that though I loved to visit Manhattan, I would never live there. Those feelings went away during that one-hour Mass. Two days later, I rented an apartment and moved to New York City a few weeks later. I selected this apartment because it has a water view of Upper New York Bay, the waterway which led ships on the final mile of their trans-Atlantic voyage to America. These ships carried more than 12 million immigrants to Ellis Island's immigrant inspection station between 1892 and 1954. After settling in New York, I started searching for work opportunities with immigrant and refugee agencies, and volunteering with outreach groups for LGBT Catholics and a Peace & Justice committee.

Alexis lived in lower Manhattan on September 11th. She had worked late the night before, so she somehow slept through all the chaos of fire truck sirens that morning. She had turned her telephone ringer and answering machine off so she could sleep late, much to the dismay of her worried family and friends. Something tells me that Alexis has been guiding me to find my next chapter in New York City.

After my spiritual awakening, I've felt as if I were flowing safely down a river. I'm not always sure of the destination, but thanks to my contemplative prayer and actions, I know I'm headed in the general direction.

.   .   .

For it is in giving that we receive. In 2005, Hurricane Katrina hit Louisiana and created hundreds of thousands of refugees, especially from New Orleans. My hometown of Austin welcomed more than 4,000 of these refugees whose homes were flooded. In Gander-like fashion, Austinites donated food, clothing, and shelter to those who were living in the Austin Convention Center. Many people helped New Orleans families who had lost everything settle in Austin. That year, the sole focus for Pay It Forward 9/11 efforts by staff was to help hurricane refugees. I also volunteered one day, signing up to help at the civic auditorium to help those with medical needs.

Austin reacted with Gander-like kindness when they helped New Orleans refugees who had been forced from their flooded homes by Hurricane Katrina.
PHOTO CREDIT: MATT CURTIS

I'll never forget meeting eighty-year-old Lysle within a few minutes of arriving at the shelter. As he was exiting the bathroom, I simply asked him how he was doing, expecting him to say, "Okay."

Instead, he said, "Not so well, I can't find my wife."

I asked him to sit down in the cafeteria so I could learn more. Lysle's wife had cancer, and she had been staying at Mercy Hospital in New Orleans when the floodwaters required all patients to be evacuated by helicopter. Unfortunately, that meant loved ones were on their own. Lysle was sent to the New Orleans Convention Center, which was hardly functioning as a working shelter. Toilets weren't working, and power was intermittent. When Lysle went to sleep that night, he took out his hearing aids and laid them on his one suitcase. Sadly, someone stole the suitcase and hearing aids while he slept. Eventually he was rescued by the National Guard, and put on a flight to Austin. When he landed, he thought he was in San Antonio. This reminded me of when I was stranded in New-foundland, when I first thought I was in Nova Scotia.

Using Gander-like inspiration, I took on the job of a social worker, trying to help him get information about his wife and connect him to his relatives. All Lysle knew was that his wife was being medevaced to a hospital in Baton Rouge. That was enough for me to start. After finding the phone number for hospitals in the city, I called and asked if his wife had been admitted from New Orleans. I got lucky on the first try. After a few minutes of explaining who I was, a nurse put his wife on the phone, and then I handed my cell phone to Lysle. He started to cry when he heard his wife's voice. It had been five days since they last spoke. She didn't know where he was, or if he was alive.

His wife reminded Lysle that he had a relative who lived in Austin. They gave me his name, so I called 411 information and was lucky enough to reach him by phone within minutes. I told him his great-uncle from New Orleans had been sent to the Austin refugee shelter. He told me that his relatives were all worried about him, not knowing where he had been sent. Within an hour, a young man had arrived at the shelter, ready to take Lysle to his apartment. The next day, I called a hearing aid company, telling them the story of Lysle and his stolen hearing aids. They said they would happily help him out by donating a new set to him. Weeks later, Lysle's wife was discharged from the hospital. Their New Orleans home was still off limits from the flood, so she came to live with Lysle in Austin for a few weeks. I was blessed to be able to witness their emotional reunion.

Americans are truly great at helping neighbors and strangers when there is a natural disaster. We need this same type of compassion year-round. Too often we let fear get in the way.

The plane people or "come from aways" stranded in Gander were temporary refugees of war. A war begun by Osama bin Laden had broken out in New York, Pennsylvania, and Washington, DC. Canadian authorities could have treated the stranded passengers as refugees with terrorists among us, leaving us on the planes for days, perhaps sending out food and water. But they didn't. Every person in Gander and the surrounding towns took a chance and offered us kindness and goodwill. They let us off the planes and took care of us in the most beautiful, loving ways.

In 2016, I asked Gander mayor Claude Elliott whether they had been nervous about permitting a terrorist from one of the planes to enter their community when they helped us on that tragic day.

"I don't think we can live our life in fear. Not everybody is out to do bad things. We have to realize that not every Muslim is a terrorist. Of course there are bad people out there, but we were willing to take that chance. We weren't going to let people suffer on those planes for four to five days. That never came into our minds. Even though we've received thousands of accolades, that's not why we did it," he said. "We just said 'thank you' and we were paid in full by knowing we helped people at a very difficult time."

Ganderite Diane Davis echoes Mayor Elliott's sentiment. "We had passengers from all over the world, but we had no conflicts or trouble," she says. "Fear and misunderstanding lead to extreme action, but they can also lead to empathy."

Would a small town in rural America welcome planes of international travelers, especially if some came from Arab countries? Some would, of course. Others would let fear rule the day, and might encourage somebody else, like the federal government, to handle the crisis.

At the Seattle performance of *Come From Away*, I was invited onstage for an audience question-and-answer session for those interested in staying longer after the show. Virtually everyone in the audience stuck around.

I was asked about how my perspective of Gander has changed me, then versus now. I replied, "During the attacks of 9/11, stranded airline passengers became temporary refugees. The Canadians didn't have to let us off the planes, but they did. Why is there so much hysteria about helping others in our country today, especially millions of Syrian war refugees?"

. . .

According to the US State Department, the US admitted 12,500 Syrian refugees out of the five million who fled their country due to the ongoing civil war.

By November 2016, the Canadian government had already resettled 44,000 Syrian refugees. I was not surprised to learn the town of Gander was again acting as a role model for compassion and empathy for Syrian refugees.

It was the unforgettable photo of Alan Kurdi, the young Syrian boy whose lifeless body washed up on a shore in Turkey, that galvanized people in Gander to step up and help refugees once again. Gander's town council organized a meeting that drew more than forty people, some of whom then formed the Gander Refugee Outreach Committee.

During a 2016 trip to Gander, I met members of the Alsayed Ali family, one of the first Syrian families adopted by Gander Refugee Outreach. PHOTO CREDIT: KEVIN TUERFF

Mayor Elliott said, "We figured opponents would show up to the meetings, but we have not had one individual with a negative view, it's only people wanting to help. We had no major objections to bringing Syrian refugees to Gander from anyone in the community. Everyone believed that if you brought in a family, we had little to fear."

When the towns of Gander and Lewisporte decided to adopt five Syrian families, the Canadian government required that they raise $15,000 per family to receive federal funds to assist the families.

Diane Davis retired from teaching and has become a full-time volunteer for Gander Refugee Outreach. Just as she did for the 9/11 come from aways, Diane is doing anything and everything she can to help the Syrian refugees resettle in Gander. She helps coordinate volunteers, soliciting supplies, arranging for medical care, and explaining Gander culture.

Diane explained how challenging it was to raise money for the effort.

"There was no single donor who could write a check. The Anglican Church was first in raising funds through bake sales and other small fund-raisers. The United Church was next in raising money for the second family. Each of these churches had other fund-raising needs, like paying for roof repair on the church." She added, "But they prioritized the families in need."

Because Gander is a small, rural town, there's a shortage of physicians. One doctor, originally from Syria, commutes to Gander to help. He happened to be on a plane with the second of five Syrian refugee families that were being welcomed in Gander.

When they arrived in the Gander Airport terminal, he witnessed an outpouring of love similar to what I saw on 9/11. The terminal was filled with people, including dozens of children, who came to welcome their new residents.

He told CBC-TV, "The first thing we saw was their little child come out … he was stunned to see all these people at two in the morning." He added, "The waiting children rushed toward the boy in welcome, as the rest of the family appeared and began to cry."

The Syrian-Canadian doctor was moved. He went on, "Here I'm helping Gander, and here Gander is helping people of the same heritage as me."

Having worked closely with the families for six months now, Diane knows a lot about Syrian refugees. She believes if more people looked at refugees as individuals and families, not statistics, they might see that we are more the same than we are different. "We both like to cook and to feed people. We both want our kids to get an education. We both want to work to support our families. If we get hurt, we cry. If we get cut, we bleed. If we tell a joke, we laugh."

One of the Muslim refugees told Diane she was impressed how the Christian church volunteers practiced their religion through good deeds rather than just words. Diane says these new Canadian residents have one year of funding from the Canadian government to find work to support their families.

The refugees want to succeed, to live without social services from the government. Right away, they have done everything from cleaning dishes at a restaurant to mowing lawns. They want to be able to volunteer in their communities to help others. They want to pay it forward.

According to Refugees International, the number of displaced persons forced from their homes globally has risen from twenty-five million to sixty-five million people from 2011 to 2015. This is a crisis that goes beyond the Syrian civil war. Thousands of people are being displaced across the globe because of changes in climate and related ability to work. When tremendous floods or droughts hit a country, it's impossible for farmers to provide for their families. They may migrate within their country to a suburban area, but then they face the challenge of finding jobs that aren't in agriculture. It's a safe bet that almost all of these refugees aren't as fortunate as we were when we were stranded in Gander. Many live in tents without running water, food, or healthcare. These challenges aren't going away. In fact, if we don't sufficiently deal with the underlying causes of forced displacement, we could see more wars, more refugees, and less peace.

When the *Come From Away* production came to Gander for two shows, Diane Davis arranged for fourteen Syrian refugees to see the show. They received VIP seats in the front row.

Unfortunately, within days of taking office, President Donald Trump called for an immediate halt to resettlement of Syrian refugees in the United States.

The kindness of strangers in Gander inspired me in 2001 and again in 2016. My faith in God and all humanity is stronger because of my experiences with Gander. Now it's my turn to champion the cause of immigrants and refugees. I have embraced my role as a channel of peace. Where there is hatred, let me bring love.

The famous Christian line "Do unto others as you would have them do unto you" (Matthew 7:12) has almost identical teachings in Buddhism, Hinduism, Judaism, and Islam. My prayer is that as countries across the globe, we can work to better understand how much we have in common. Differences in gender, race, religion, political party, or sexual orientation shouldn't draw battle lines between the human race. We need each other to coexist in peace.

CHAPTER 9

Ten Tips for Encouraging Kindness

Inspired by the Pay It Forward Foundation, EnviroMedia staff performed
random acts of kindness on each anniversary of 9/11. We often learned how
the giver receives more than the recipient. IMAGE CREDIT: KEVIN TUERFF

In 2009, the US Congress and President Barack Obama
joined together to pass bipartisan national service legislation
that formally designated September 11th as a National Day of

Service and Remembrance. Canada enacted the same in 2011. There are many organizations, including 911Day.org and cndsfoundation.ca, that offer ideas and resources to participate. "Never forget" must not get lost as a social media hashtag as the years go by. Consider some act of personal or community service on the next anniversary.

In June 2017, President Trump recognized me as founder of Pay It Forward 9/11, and Jay Winuk, the co-founder of 911Day.org at the Ford's Theatre Society Gala in Washington. He said, "We're incredibly inspired to hear the amazing work that Kevin Tuerff and Jay Winuk have done with Pay It Forward 9/11 and 9/11 Day. From one of the darkest days in American history, these citizens have carried forward a spirit of service, charity and love of our country."

That same month, the new September 11th Families' Association honored the sixteen years of Pay It Forward 9/11 by including a video and photo about the effort in its *Seeds of Service* exhibit at the new 9/11 Tribute Museum in New York City.

People can be nervous about approaching strangers to do a good deed as a random act of kindness. You might try it any day of the year. But each year on September 11th, an easy way to start a conversation with a stranger is to say, "Hello, today is the anniversary of the September 11th attacks, and I'm part of a group doing good deeds to honor the lives lost and heroes who helped others on 9/11. I'd like to give you _____, and if you'd like to, you might continue the movement by doing the same for another stranger you meet."

Nine times out of ten, people open up and smile, accepting whatever small token of kindness with gratitude. Sometimes they get excited and immediately look around for another stranger they might help the same way.

Now you know what to say, but perhaps you need ideas on what and where you might try to participate on September 11th or any other day of the year. Here are a few:

1.
THANK FIRST RESPONDERS

Many people show their appreciation for police, fire, and EMS workers on the anniversary of 9/11 because so many were lost in rescue efforts at the World Trade Center. Our staff frequently visited a fire or police station, offering various gifts, usually food.

In Portland, Oregon, one staff team visited the administrative office of a fire department, people who are often overlooked, and provided them with a free lunch. Breakfast tacos were delivered one year to new firefighter cadets who were in the middle of training for climbing the stairs of tall buildings with heavy equipment.

One way to thank first responders, which only costs the price of a postage stamp, is to write thank-you notes to military, police, fire, and EMS personnel. In Nashville, one teacher made this part of a civics lesson, assigning each seventh-grader to write these letters, which were then mailed by the school to nearby offices.

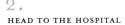

2.

HEAD TO THE HOSPITAL

Over the years, several Pay It Forward teams have gone to hospitals to perform random acts of kindness. In the maternity ward, savings bonds were given in the names of newborns born on September 11th, so their birthday would be remembered in a positive way—as often these gifts are 9/11 memorials. One employee went to a hospital, explained her mission, and asked where the greatest need was.

The hospital told her that there was a woman there who had lived in New York on 9/11. She was a grandmother raising the child of a parent who may have died in the World Trade Center. The grandmother cried tears of joy after accepting a cash gift and a card. She said that she would continue the effort by paying it forward to someone else. Another staffer went to the cancer ward and gave some money to a woman waiting for chemotherapy treatment.

3.

FIND OUT WHAT YOUR LOCAL SCHOOL NEEDS

Usually it just takes one quick phone call to a school principal to find someone who would appreciate a hundred-dollar gift. At one school, two low-income kids recently had their bicycles stolen. The parents couldn't afford to replace them, and the kids had to walk a long distance to school. Two bikes were delivered that day.

Another elementary school principal explained that the school had installed a new garden, but they needed gardening tools. Rakes, shovels, hoes, and gloves were purchased and delivered that day.

A similar request for help in the garden came from a different school, which really needed mulch. The principal arranged for nearly 300 kids to assemble outside at the garden. After explaining to the children about the importance of remembering those who died on 9/11, and the story of Gander's kindness, our employee pulled out a hundred-dollar bill and explained that one child would receive this money to use for their own Pay It Forward 9/11. Several kids shared their ideas for helping others, and one was chosen to receive the prize.

Often, my staff would go beyond donating with the company's money and chip in money of their own. One team arranged to purchase a dump truck full of mulch for the school garden. On cue, they yelled, "Bring on the mulch!" The truck pulled around and dumped the mulch at the garden site. The kids went wild, screaming with delight. Over mulch! A teacher told our team, "I saw a story on the news about this effort, and I said to myself, I wish that would happen to my school. And it did!"

4.

A CUP OF COFFEE OR A SANDWICH GOES FAR

Since the *Pay It Forward* movie, many news stories have been written about random good deeds. There was a news story of a Starbucks in Florida at which a woman gave additional money to the cashier, telling them to pay for the coffee of the person behind her in line. That person was so surprised, they said, "I'll keep it going, use my money to pay for the person behind me." And it kept on going, and going, and going for eleven hours. In the end, 378 people had paid for a stranger's coffee.

During our Pay It Forward 9/11 events, many people visited coffee shops or food trucks to plunk down $20 or more to pay for coffees or sandwiches ordered by the next random customers. Sometimes, our staffers would stand there and explain why we were doing this. Other times, they would sit back across the room and watch the reactions of people after they had their coffee or sandwich paid for by a stranger. A smile bloomed on each customer's face, every time. One of our staffers purchased a Starbucks gift card and put $50 on it. They gave it to a random customer and told them to pay for someone else's coffee, and to invite that person to continue doing the same, until the card ran out of money. Eight months later, I received a phone call from a nonprofit executive who was familiar with our company and our annual tradition.

She said, "You won't believe what happened to me today. I was meeting a potential new donor for coffee. When I went to purchase it, the person I was meeting with handed me a Starbucks gift card. The woman said, 'Oh, I'm supposed to buy your coffee using this gift card. It's some sort of pay it forward thing.' I told her, 'I know where this came from. It started months ago on September 11th.' My guess is that people added money to the card when the balance went low, which kept the free coffees flowing for months."

5.

LOOK FOR IDEAS IN THE CRAIGSLIST "WANTED" SECTION

One team went to Craigslist and found an ad about a battered woman living in a women's shelter after leaving a twenty-year abusive relationship. She had nothing. She was using a Thomas the Train comforter for her bed. So they bought her a nice, new comforter. They also bought her beauty and bath products to pamper herself. On Craigslist, I searched the term "wanted" under the General Community section. I found that some people had simple requests like a ride across town. Another post, titled "In desperate need," was a person who lost their job unexpectedly and needed help purchasing Christmas presents for his son. This person wrote, "I am at the point where I don't know what to do, and don't have anywhere to turn."

Is it an online scam? I doubt it.

6.

THANK AIRLINE INDUSTRY WORKERS

Anyone who flies in airplanes for a living, or works at an airport, knows there is the threat of a copycat terror attack on the anniversary of 9/11. One year, I happened to be on another international flight, traveling from Tokyo to New York. I didn't have time to purchase anything before getting aboard the flight. Thankfully, our large jumbo jet came with its own duty-free shop. I saw that they had red, white, and blue jelly beans for sale. I purchased one box for each of the twelve flight attendants and wrote a note explaining why I was doing this. Over the course of the flight, each of the flight attendants came by my seat to personally thank me for thinking of them in this small way.

One staffer thought a lot about flight crews and thanking them for their service on the anniversary. Back in 2002, before the widespread popularity of cell phones, many pilots used long-distance calling cards. She bought and distributed debit cards to several pilots in uniform as they arrived at the airport. She once provided snacks to cashiers who worked at airport parking lot toll booths. Another year, she contacted the director of Austin's FAA flight control tower and explained that she wanted to bring a cake to the air traffic controllers on duty that day.

7.
GIVE AWAY FLOWERS TO BRIGHTEN SOMEONE'S DAY

At the famous Pike Place Market in Seattle, one team purchased dozens of daisies and proceeded to hand them out one-by-one to random shoppers, along with a small note card explaining, "SMILE. You're the recipient of a random act of kindness." There were dozens of smiles in the market that day. In Portland, one team went to a local florist and picked up the tab for a man buying roses for his girlfriend. He was touched and pledged to pay it forward.

8.

HELP SOCIAL SERVICE AGENCIES

Many groups have supported a local battered women's shelter, a refugee outreach group, a foster home, a teen drug and alcohol rehabilitation center, a hospice, or a food bank. After you decide which agency to support, call in advance and ask for a manager. Explain what you're trying to do and ask what items they might need. Often, they need simple items and the money for them just isn't in their budget. One teen rehab center wanted colored pencils and candy. A Ronald McDonald temporary residence for the parents of children in the hospital needed detergent for its washing-machine room. A hospice wanted current magazines for loved ones visiting patients to read in the lobby. A homeless shelter wanted men's white tube socks. A VA hospital wanted transit passes to help low-income veterans get to their appointments. A blood bank—well, you know what they needed.

9.

FEED THE METER; FEED THE VENDING MACHINE

For cities that still have parking meters that require coins, it's easy to add a quarter or more to someone's parking meter that has expired or is about to expire. Many of our staff did this over the years. Most likely you won't get the opportunity to witness the recipient's reaction to this good deed. They may not even realize they were at risk of getting a parking ticket. You might add a note to the windshield explaining the concept of Pay It Forward. One person went further, going to traffic court to pay for the parking tickets of strangers.

Be creative! There are transportation-related deeds you can do. Anyone waiting at a bus shelter or subway station would appreciate a free transit pass. Thousands of college students ride their bikes to class. Most people have a water bottle rack on their bike, and most of the time it's empty. One team bought a few cases of bottled water and went from bike rack to bike rack, adding a water bottle to bicycles. Who wouldn't like a free bottle of water to quench their thirst, especially if you commute by pedal power?

Sometimes, we provided free snacks or candy to college students. Dollar bills were taped to the front of several vending machines on campus, including a note about Pay It Forward.

10.

DO SOMETHING THAT BRINGS YOU GREAT JOY

There are countless opportunities to bring joy to others through a random act of kindness. They don't have to cost money, but a small donation can go a long way. If you've never tried doing random acts of kindness, but you want to, put some thought into something that really connects with you. Did someone or some organization help you along the way at some point in your life?

In 2000, Shelly received the gift of life from a random stranger: a new kidney from an anonymous organ donor who passed away. Diagnosed with diabetes at age twenty, she was going to receive a kidney donated by her father. When it came time for his surgery, doctors found that his kidney had cancer. Her father was successfully treated for cancer, and Shelly received the beautiful gift of a new kidney from an organ donor, a stranger who died unexpectedly. In 2005, Shelly contributed her company Pay It Forward donation to the Texas Renal Coalition, a local kidney healthcare organization. She has served the organization ever since. More importantly, she used her time at the post-event staff meeting to explain the importance of organ donation. She also passed out printed information about the Donate Life campaign to staff members, encouraging them to become organ donors. Her story moved me and others to sign up with the state organ donor registry.

One staffer decided he wanted to do something nice for his childhood cello instructor. He felt his life was changed by learning and appreciating music. On September 11th, he showed up at the music school and found his same instructor, still teaching after twenty years. He donated money to the school so that a low-income student could receive a few music lessons from that instructor. Tears were shed. Joy happened. Kindness was spread to a stranger.

. . .

These random acts of kindness are just one ripple in the enormous ocean of goodwill that our friends in Gander taught us. As Mayor Elliott expressed many times in his humble interviews for the news media, "We saw the best of humanity and the worst of humanity on the very same day."

It was almost too much for the come from aways to absorb as it was happening, but the experience changed our lives forever. And, it's the kind of love that the world needs in order to heal. Not the romantic or familial love that we all know, but rather a love for humanity. After all, isn't that what we're here for?

In 2016, Mayor Elliott said, "Love, compassion, and understanding: That is what the world is lacking today. If Gander's story can help someone, then we need to tell it over and over again."

Consider putting down your electronic devices now and then, to look up at strangers to truly see them. I'd like to see the words "Look Up and Gander" become a social movement where people who learn the 9/11 story of Gander, Newfoundland, go out and practice acts of kindness to strangers on a regular basis. If younger generations take the lead, perhaps others will continue the flow of kindness through the channel of peace that began on September 11, 2001.

When Your 9/11 Story Becomes a Broadway Musical

Tony-nominated American Theater actor Chad Kimball plays the character Kevin T., inspired by the experiences of Kevin Tuerff (r) in the Broadway musical *Come From Away*. PHOTO CREDIT: KEVIN TUERFF

I never expected that my story of being a 9/11 refugee, and the stories of many others who had similar experiences, would ultimately be told in the Broadway musical *Come From Away.* Or that a younger, better-looking, and immensely talented Tony-nominated actor-singer would play me onstage.

Actor Chad Kimball was asked how he feels when the person he portrays, his doppelgänger, is in the audience (me). He said, "If we were to do an imitation it would come off differently. Our director, Chris Ashely, gave us carte blanche to create the characters under the auspices of the true story. So, I knew all about Kevin before we met, but I was able to create Kevin T. anew." Chad and I have become friends and occasionally meet for dinner. He's not bothered playing a gay character even though he is straight. I shared with him how times have changed in entertainment's portrayal of LGBT characters.

On the tenth anniversary of the terror attacks on America, David Hein and Irene Sankoff, the husband-and-wife team from Toronto who wrote the book, lyrics, and music for *Come From Away,* interviewed me about my experiences in Gander. We met at the College of the North Atlantic, on my first return trip back to my 9/11 shelter. They interviewed me several times over the next year via Skype. Then, in 2013, I traveled to Sheridan College in Toronto, Canada, to see the first version of the show performed. Although the show blew me away, I assumed the musical would end with that college production. Instead, it was a snowball that gathered speed and support along the way in San Diego, Seattle, Washington, DC, Gander, and Toronto. Then in 2017, the show debuted at the Schoenfeld Theatre on Broadway.

In Tony-Award winning *Come From Away,* Kevin T.—my

character—begins the song "Prayer," which is based in part on the Christian hymn "Make Me a Channel of Your Peace." After watching on TV the continuous loop of video of planes crashing into the World Trade Center in 2001, this song played in my head in the days after 9/11. As a member of Generation X, I grew up primarily in a time of peace, where Americans were not engaged in war with another country. This hymn is based on the Prayer of St. Francis, which extols the simple virtues of peace, love, and kindness to all.

But how could my doppelgänger be singing this onstage if I never told anyone that this hymn had run through my mind? I didn't remember telling David and Irene.

When I first heard the song "Prayer" in the musical, I couldn't breathe. It was like someone had sucker punched me. In the play, that song in my head begins a litany that's joined by the voices of other characters, adding Jewish, Muslim, and Hindu prayers about peace in song.

Michael Rubinoff, who first commissioned *Come From Away* for the Canadian Music Theatre Project at Sheridan College, shared an email with me from his friend Paul Akins, who had seen the full production. Paul wrote, "I was bolted back into my Catholic childhood when 'Make Me a Channel of Your Peace' began. It's a song that helped shape who I am today, but it also made me run for the hills when the Catholic Church made me feel shameful when I was a young gay man. The song tonight made me look at life differently. It allowed me to forgive, accept, and move on. What a brilliant piece of theater—especially that very moving scene!"

Wow. Through the beauty of storytelling, fifteen years after a hymn went through my head, I was able to connect with a stranger just like me, a gay Catholic struggling to remain faithful to an unwelcoming church.

When I came out of the closet at twenty-two, I was blessed by finding a support group of other gay Catholics in Austin, Texas. Because that group helped me realize that my identity and my faith could be consistent with each other, I remain an active member of the Catholic Church. Almost all my LGBT friends have left the Church due to hate speech from the Vatican and other Church leaders. I jokingly told others that I was "the last gay Catholic with my foot in the door." I hoped for change eventually, and I tried to change hearts and minds by being visible while providing leadership, service, and financial support to my church. I'm happy Pope Francis has begun to heal the wounds of the past with welcoming comments like this: "If a person is gay and seeks out the Lord and is willing, who am I to judge that person?"

Even better, Pope Francis has said that gays and lesbians are owed an apology by the Church, who has offended them.

On the fifteenth anniversary of the 9/11 attacks, many US communities had dialed-back ceremonies commemorating the lives lost. In Washington, DC, the leaders at Ford's Theatre believed this musical was exactly what their audience needed to see right then because of the political divisions.

It was surreal to find myself sitting near the front row of this historic theater, the place where President Abraham Lincoln was assassinated. I'd worked for years in Washington, DC, but I had never been inside the theater, which is also a national historic site. The presidential box seats are empty, with a framed portrait of President George Washington facing the stage. Ford's Theatre celebrates the legacy of President

Lincoln and explores the American experience through theater and education.

Before the show began, I was introduced along with a
handful of others whose stories are portrayed in the show. I
thought, *Is this really happening?*

As I looked around the theater, I couldn't believe I was
sitting amid some of the most high-profile political leaders
in the country. Directly in front of me was Andrew Card, the
chief of staff to President George W. Bush. He's the man who
whispered to President Bush that America was under attack
as the president read to schoolchildren in Florida. Sitting in
the front row was the US secretary of the interior Sally Jew-
ell, appointed by President Obama. Behind me was Republican Senator Roy Blunt from Missouri. Across the aisle were
Senators Susan Collins, a Republican from Maine, and former
Senate Majority Leader Harry Reid, a Democrat from Nevada.
Since I'd already seen the show three times, I decided to watch
how these political leaders from both parties reacted to *Come
From Away*. Guess what? They all laughed and cried throughout the entire performance. It didn't matter what political
party you were in, this show was uniting people, reminding
everyone of the power, beauty, and importance of kindness
to strangers. After the show, I shook hands with Andrew Card
and thanked him for his service on that tragic day. I disagreed
with the decisions of Mr. Card and President Bush, taking our
country into war in Iraq. Perhaps this show could unite us all
back to a time of peace.

Before the opening of the musical in Washington DC, I
was invited to a welcome reception at the Canadian Embassy
to the United States. David MacNaughton, the Canadian

ambassador, told the guests and patrons from Ford's Theatre that "On that tragic day, Canadians lent a hand to their neighbor. No thanks are necessary. The debt is paid in full."

Gander mayor Claude Elliott added, "We just do good deeds and cherish the memories."

After the September 11th show in Washington, DC, I woke up to see a newspaper slipped underneath my hotel room door. On the front page of the Metro section of the *Washington Post* was the headline "Stranded on 9/11, a small town in Canada showed him kindness. This is how he pays it forward," written by Colby Itkowitz, the *Inspired Life* blog writer for the *Post*. The writer described how I'd been true to remembering the anniversary of the attacks by encouraging kindness to strangers, and highlighted some generous actions the cast and crew of the musical had taken the previous day.

A month later, I was invited by the show's producers to join the cast and crew on their trip to Gander, Newfoundland, for a benefit performance of *Come From Away*. It's not an easy trip to get to Gander because there are no direct flights from America. I met up with a group of eighty people at LaGuardia Airport for a long day's journey, flying northwest to Toronto, then east to St. John's, Newfoundland. From there, it was a late-night four-hour bus ride to the town of Gander.

I'll never forget my 2016 Gander trip. I was reunited with friends who had been my 9/11 caretakers. At the Gander Airport, I also met Bruce Heyman, the US ambassador to Canada. He presented a beautiful bronze plaque, offering gratitude on behalf of the United States to the people of Gander and the surrounding towns for the role they played in taking care of the more than 6,500 stranded airline passengers for up to five days.

The actors, musicians, and crew were all nervous about performing the show for Gander's residents. They wanted to be sure they were authentic in the story, sentiment, and Newfoundland accents.

Mayor Claude Elliott shut down the town's hockey rink (that's huge!) to accommodate 2,500 people for each of the two performances. Roughly half of the town saw the musical in Gander that day, and they absolutely loved it. They cheered, laughed, cried, sang, and danced throughout. It was the blessing that everyone related to the show was looking for before going on to Toronto and Broadway in New York City.

For the opening night on Broadway, March 12, 2017, *Come From Away* producers generously brought all the doppelgangers portrayed in the show to New York City. It was great to see my friends from Gander. My ex-partner Evan was there too, and we shook hands and talked for the first time in more than seven years. Then we all joined the actors who portray us and walked out on stage during the curtain call. Although we hadn't sung a note or danced, we were told to take a bow before a rousing standing ovation. It was an unforgettable moment.

On June 11, 2017, *Come From Away* won a Tony® award from the American Theater Wing for best direction. They recognized director Christopher Ashley for his remarkable ability to tell the story of the plane people and the local Newfoundlanders with just 12 actors, using 12 chairs and two tables. I was there at Radio City Music Hall, joining Beverley Bass and Tom Stawicki and Nick and Diane Marson. We were excited the story of Gander on 9/11 was reaching millions via the awards show telecast. The show will have a long run on Broadway, and there are plans for multiple touring companies

. . .

When I met the show's writers in 2011, none of us knew how timely the message for *Come From Away* would soon become. Since then, I fear there has been a resurgence of people who fear or hate foreigners, people from different cultures, or strangers. Civil wars, climate change, and religious conflicts have caused the world's refugee crisis to grow, and people are struggling with how to handle strangers in need.

Keep hope alive by doing good deeds for strangers and supporting public policy that provides help for global refugees.

ACKNOWLEDGMENTS

The inspiration for this book comes from my involvement in sharing my story for the Broadway musical *Come From Away*. I'm grateful to Michael Rubinoff, associate dean of the Canadian Musical Theater Project at Sheridan College in Toronto. It was his idea to write a musical about Gander, Newfoundland's response to September 11, 2001. Like me, he believed what happened in Gander on 9/11 needed to be told. Michael recruited the successful husband and wife writing team of David Hein and Irene Sankoff. As a result of the Canadian government providing an arts grant, David and Irene traveled to Newfoundland for a month to fully research the story. Their hard work resulted in the book, lyrics, and music in *Come From Away*. This musical catapulted from Sheridan College to Broadway's Schoenfeld Theater in 2017 thanks to the producers from Junkyard Dog Productions, La Jolla Playhouse, the Seattle Rep Theater, and the amazing cast and crew.

In my career, I'm grateful for everyone at EnviroMedia who helped Valerie Salinas-Davis and me create and grow that business. Their loyalty and hard work allowed us to help clients improve public health and the environment while finding ways to demonstrate our commitment to philanthropic efforts like Pay it Forward 9/11. I'm grateful to Catherine Ryan Hyde for writing *Pay It Forward* and starting a foundation to encourage random acts of kindness.

I thank God for giving me an amazing family, especially my parents James and Julie Tuerff. Their unwavering love and support has been a source of constant encouragement. I also appreciate the encouragement of my three brothers and their families: Brian and Jana Tuerff; Jeff and Lynn Tuerff; Greg and Jayne Tuerff; and eight remarkable nieces and nephews.

I am grateful to these friends for their help and support with this book: Mark Aitala and Sara Beechner, Kevin Burns, Diane Davis, Claude Elliott, Dan and Melanie Fish, Sue Frost, Rebecca Geier, David Hein and Irene Sankoff, Kitten Howard, Chad Kimball, Margaret Lee, John Markey, O.P., Nick and Diane Marson, Mac and Nellie Moss, Maureen Murray and Sue Riccardelli, Michael Rubinoff, Sean Price, Michael Staffieri, Tom Stawicki and Beverly Bass, Todd Savage, Brett Will Taylor, and Ron and Sue Walsh.

I am also grateful for my team at River Grove Books and Greenleaf Book Group, including Hobbs Allison, AprilJo Murphy, Daniel Pederson, and Brian Phillips.

ABOUT THE AUTHOR

Kevin Tuerff is the CEO of Kevin Tuerff Consulting LLC, a public relations and marketing practice. In 1997, Kevin cofounded EnviroMedia, the first integrated marketing agency dedicated solely to improving public health and the environment. He is a social entrepreneur, speaker, and author with over twenty-five years of experience in marketing and public affairs.

Tuerff is passionate about the planet and its people, donating time to a number of organizations that support the cause. For fifteen years, he organized a kindness initiative to commemorate the anniversary of 9/11. In 2016, he received an

outstanding leadership award from the University of Texas Environmental Science Institute for his eight years of volunteer service. For four years, he was an elected director of a water utility,

PHOTO CREDIT: CHRIS SO, GETTY IMAGES

where he championed water conservation programs during an extreme drought.

As president of EnviroMedia, he was a cofounder of America Recycles Day, and helped Daimler launch an innovative car-sharing service across North America. Tuerff also helped the state of Texas prevent death and disease through public health behavior change campaigns.

Tuerff has a BS from the University of Texas at Austin and has lived in Austin for more than thirty years.

CPSIA information can be obtained
at www.ICGtesting.com
Printed in the USA
LVOW11s2144131017
552311LV00001B/3/P